Physical Feats That Made History

Physical Feats That Made History

HAROLD H. HART

Illustrated by Frank Kramer

HART PUBLISHING COMPANY, INC.
NEW YORK CITY

COPYRIGHT © 1974

HART PUBLISHING COMPANY, INC., NEW YORK, N.Y. 10003
ISBN NO. 08055-1118-0 (Paperback: 08055-0175-4)
LIBRARY OF CONGRESS CATALOG CARD NO. 73-82003

MANUFACTURED IN THE UNITED STATES OF AMERICA

CONTENTS

Physical Feats That Made History

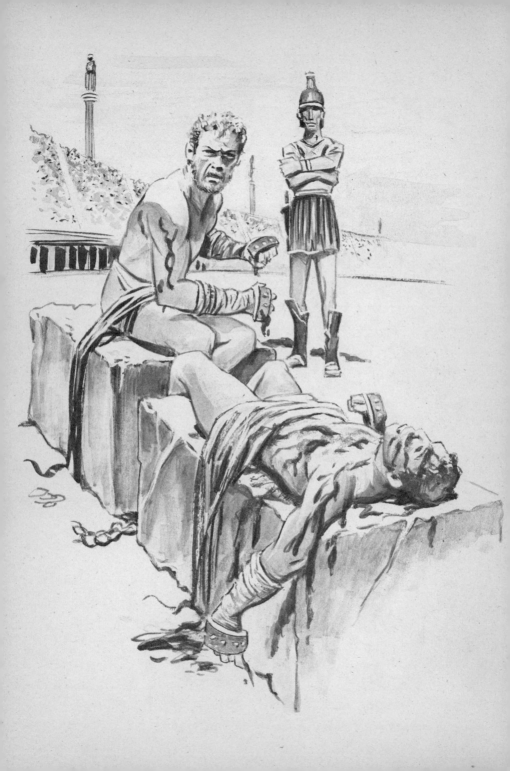

900 B.C. Theogenes fights and kills 1,425 opponents

In ancient days, the rulers of Greece and Rome would amuse themselves and their subjects through gladiatorial combats in which men fought to the death for the amusement of the spectators. History records that the greatest of these gladiators was a Greek called Theogenes, a native of Thasos.

Theogenes served a cruel prince named Thesus, who reigned about 900 B.C. Thesus delighted in sadistic spectacles and ordained a combat that was especially vicious. The two contestants—if they can be called such— were placed facing each other, almost nose to nose, each on a flat stone. Both men were strapped into place. Their fists were encased in leather thongs which were studded with small, sharp metal spikes. At a given signal, they would strike at each other, and the combat would continue, without rest, until one of the contestants had been beaten to death.

During a long career, Theogenes—strong, skillful and savage—faced 1,425 men and killed every one of them.

Source: "The Encyclopedia of Sports"; Frank G. Menke; A. S. Barnes; 1963; page ???

540 B.C.

Milo of Crotona carries an ox on his shoulders across the stadium at Olympia

The greatest wrestler and strong man of the ancient world was a Greek named Milon, who hailed from the southern Italian city of Croton, a Greek colony founded in the 8th century B.C. by settlers from Achaea. He is more commonly known by the Latin form of his name: Milo of Crotona.

Milo was a man of diversified interests and attainments. Skilled as a soldier and singer, he was a favorite disciple of the famous philosopher-mathematician Pythagoras, and he was

himself the author of the *Physica,* a book on science and natural history. But above all, Milo was renowned as an athlete. His specialties were wrestling and feats of strength.

Milo won the wrestling championship at each of the six meetings of the Olympic Games between 540 and 516 B.C., the only man in the history of the ancient Olympics (776 B.C. to A.D. 393) to win so many victories in any sport. Milo's achievement becomes even more impressive when one notes that his active career as a wrestler covered more than 24 years, an extremely long time for an athlete to maintain himself at a championship peak.

Milo's amazing feats are recorded in the writings of such

reliable ancient historians as Pausanias, Plutarch, and Strabo. According to their reports, Milo's fingers were so powerful that no one could bend them when he extended his hand horizontally. On one occasion, Milo enclosed a tender pomegranate in his mighty fist. Scores of other athletes tried to get it away from him but none succeeded. When Milo finally opened his hand, there was not the slightest bruise on the fruit.

Milo is best known, however, for a feat he performed on the opening day of one of the meetings of the Olympic Games. Carrying a full-grown ox on his shoulders—the ox must have weighed at least a ton—Milo strolled effortlessly into the stadium at Olympia. Before the amazed eyes of thousands, he carried the ox across the playing field. The story goes on to say that he slaughtered the ox, which he may have, but the legend that he ate all the meat on that same day seems somewhat apocryphal.

Source: "The Ancient Olympic Games"; Heinz Schobel; D. Van Nostrand Company; 1966; pages 54, 75–77, 100. Encyclopaedia Britannica.

490 B.C.

Pheidippides runs from Marathon to Athens

In September of 490 B.C., King Darius, the ruler of the powerful Persian Empire, sent his army to attack the city-state of Athens. His forces landed on the plain of Marathon, just a few miles from Athens.

Though greatly outnumbered, the Athenians marched out to meet the invaders, while sending a request for help to their allies in Sparta. The message was carried by Pheidippides, the best runner in Athens.

Racing out of the city on foot, he ran all that day and through the night, forging ahead across rough, rocky terrain in which the road was often barely suitable for mules and mountain goats. The next morning, having covered a distance of 140 miles, he arrived in Sparta. After delivering his message and getting the answer, he set out to rejoin the Athenian troops, once again covering the distance in a day and a night.

Just a few days later, the Athenian and Persian armies clashed in the now famous battle of Marathon. Though he'd had only a short time to rest up from his magnificent two-way run, Pheidippides participated in the battle as an infantryman.

Contrary to expectations, the Athenians decisively defeated the Persians. Like his fellow soldiers, who had fought so hard against the numerically superior enemy, Pheidippides was exhausted when the fighting came to an end. Nonetheless, he gamely accepted the Athenian commander's request to carry the news of the victory to the anxious inhabitants of the city. Casting off his heavy armor, the exhausted Pheidippides

set out on his last and greatest run.

The distance from Marathon to Athens is 22 miles 1,470 yards. Pheidippides covered it in just a few hours, but the ordeal was too much for his already overtaxed system. Shouting, "Victory, victory" with his last breaths, he staggered into the central marketplace of Athens, then dropped to the pavement—dead.

The Athenians never forgot this noble patriotic sacrifice; and in the years that followed, they established a series of memorial games, including running events of various kinds, in memory of Pheidippides. When the Olympic Games were

revied in 1896, a road-race called the marathon was made
a regular event. In 1924, its distance was standardized
at 26 miles 385 yards.

Source: "The Histories"; Herodotus; Book 6. Encyclopaedia Britannica.

1389 Three knights take on all comers for an entire month of jousting

The characteristic athletic competition of the Middle Ages was the joust, a contest in which two fully armored knights mounted on horseback would engage in mock combat with lances.

Because the rules of jousting varied in different places and times, and because there was no attempt at formal record-keeping, it is impossible today to identify those knights who might be considered the jousting champions of their era. Nonetheless, the works of medieval historians provide accounts of many outstanding feats.

Perhaps the most impressive is the exploit of three chamberlains at the court of King Charles VI of France—Sir Boucicaut the Younger, Sir Reginald de Roye, and the Lord de Saimpi.

During the winter of the year 1389, these three knights sent heralds throughout Europe to proclaim a daring challenge. For 30 days, beginning on May 31st, they would hold a field of arms on the plain of St. Inglevere, outside Calais, against all comers.

As news of this challenge spread, knights from all over Europe began pouring into Calais. Among the first to arrive was a party of 60 English knights led by Sir John Holland, the half-brother of King Richard II.

On the morning of May 21, 1389, in accordance with the announced rules of the tournament, the three French knights, mounted and fully armed, were waiting in the lists at St. Inglevere. The contest began with a joust between Sir Boucicaut and Sir John, the most prominent of the English challengers. The two knights met at full gallop, impacting

with such force that the French knight's lance, though safely blunted with a coronel, pierced the Englishman's shield and bruised his arm. Course after course of jousting followed, as each of the 60 English knights tried his luck against the three Frenchmen.

After a week or so of tilting, the Englishmen returned home vanquished. In the days and weeks that followed, the three valiant French knights continued to hold their own against numerous challengers from other countries. When the 30 days elapsed, they were still in honorable possession of the field—a feat of chivalry so outstanding that King Charles awarded them a prize of 10,000 francs.

Source: "The Chronicles of England, France, and Spain"; Sir John Froissart, 1400; Book IV, chapter xx.

1764 Powell walks 50 miles in seven hours

In 1764, Foster Powell set off from London by foot for the town of Bath. The famous seaside resort was 50 miles away, over cobblestone and dirt roads.

It took the 30-year-old barrister from Leeds a mere seven hours to reach his destination. Powell had walked at a rate of better than seven miles an hour!

By comparison, consider that today a good marathon racer requires almost two and one-half hours to run 26 miles over a smoothly paved track.

Source: "Curiosities of Human Nature"; S. G. Goodrich; J. S. Locke & Co.; 1876; page 305.

1809 Barclay walks 1,000 miles in 1,000 hours—one mile every hour

Captain Allardyce Barclay of Ury, Scotland, was veritably a man with "asbestos feet." At age 17, he could walk six miles an hour. At age 27, he claimed that he could walk 1,000 miles in 1,000 hours. A group of Englishmen didn't believe this incredible Scot, and offered odds of 100 to 1 against Barclay's boast.

In June 1, 1809, Captain Allardyce Barclay lined up ready to go the distance. The terms of the wager called for him to walk one mile within each of the next consecutive 1,000 hours. The mile was to be covered regardless of weather. The hours were to be counted uninterruptedly. He would be obliged to walk day and night one-half mile down a path from his own lodgings in Newmarket and then walk the same half-mile back to his home. Barclay had undertaken a stint that would keep him going without a decent sleep for roughly six weeks. It seemed utterly impossible that any man would have the endurance to do this.

Surprisingly, the lack of rest was not the Captain's major problem. Barclay devised a system of walking the first mile at the very end of a rest period. He then immediately commenced to do a second mile at the very beginning of the following hour. Since each mile took him approximately 15 minutes, this arrangement permitted him to rest for several 1½-hour periods each day. But Barclay began suffering from muscle spasms and blisters. Moreover, there was grave concern that the wearied

contestant might be the victim of foul play on the dark road, for a good deal of money was being bet against him. His brother arranged to have the pathway lit at night.

During those summer days, the road became hot and dusty. Ingeniously, Barclay had a water cart sprinkle the path in front of him. In between times, he cheerfully indulged in solid meals of mutton chops and beefsteaks, washed down by generous drafts of port wine.

At the start, Barclay required only approximately 13 minutes for each mile; but after four weeks of steady perambulating, he was worn to a frazzle. As he plowed through his miles in 20 minutes each, the odds against him grew. But Barclay, half-dead, struggled on.

Strangely enough, as he approached the finish, he actually gained strength. During the last few days, ropes were needed to hold back the crowd, and lords and commoners filled every available room in the Newmarket area. Many were bettors who, in the aggregate, had staked $500,000 against Barclay.

On July 12, Barclay finished his last mile. The final chore took him a mere 15 minutes, and he wound up 45 minutes ahead of schedule. It was like dashing for a pot of gold, for Barclay had bet a very considerable sum on himself. In winning, he became a wealthy man, in addition to establishing a record for human endurance that is probably unmatched.

Source: The Times of London; July 14, 1809; page 3, column 1.

1831 Osbaldeston rides horseback for 200 miles in eight hours and 42 minutes

George Osbaldeston was a 155-pound jockey who operated the Newmarket Inn. He was known as "The Squire." On November 5, 1831, George announced that he would ride horseback for 200 miles in less than 10 hours over a Newmarket track. To back his words, Osbaldeston

put up 1,000 guineas in cash, a considerable sum
in those days.

The terms of the bet were that the rider could change
horses (he would ride one horse for four miles and then
switch to another horse), that he could use the same horse
two or more times, that all elapsed time—whether used
for riding, mounting, or resting — would be counted, and
that if a horse failed to last a distance for any cause
whatsoever, that would just be too bad and Osbaldeston
would lose.

The race would take place on a set Saturday, regardless
of the weather.

Days before the race, Newmarket was crowded with racing
fans. On Saturday, November 5, 1831, as per agreement,
the ground was measured at Newmarket's Round Course.
George would mount at Duke's Stand, where many celebrities
had gathered to watch, and he would go the four-mile
distance around the track, ending up at Duke's Stand

to mount another horse. "The Squire" would do 50 laps.

A fresh lamb-skin-covered saddle would be ready for George every time he arrived for a new mount. So would refreshments, including porridge, warm jelly, and weak brandy. A change of clothing was also laid out, but Osbaldeston did not require it.

The hazards were many: a lame horse could slow him down; an injured horse could ruin the day; an accident to himself would be the supreme disaster. Thundershowers threatened to turn the track into a quagmire; and in fact, it did rain all day long. But the dauntless jockey, clad in a purple silk jacket and doeskin breeches, was off and running at 7:12 a.m. He made it around the first four miles in the good time of nine minutes flat. *Clasher*, his 10th horse, broke down near Duke's Stand, but Osbaldeston nursed it home. His 13th mount, *Coroner*, used for a second time, turned in an 8:40 clocking. His 21st mount, Fury, negotiated the track in 8:10. Without question, "The Squire" was running well as the race neared the halfway point.

After a six-minute rest period, on round No. 31, the jockey ran into his first setback. *Ikie Solomons* tripped and threw him, but Osbaldeston held onto the reins and managed to avoid serious mishap. Still, the accident cost him about four minutes' time.

Now the rain began to fall faster. By the 48th round, horse and rider were both mercilessly drenched by a driving torrent. One of "The Squire's" mounts actually did turn around on the track and try to run back to shelter. But George braved on.

As he crossed the finish line, Osbaldeston drew a mighty cheer. He had spent seven hours, 19 minutes, four seconds on his horses, and another one hour, 22 minutes and 56 seconds mounting and resting. His total elapsed time—eight hours and 42 minutes—was well under the allowed 10 hours of his bet.

However, "The Squire" hadn't had enough. After he rode home on his favorite horse, he penned a letter to *The Times of London* offering to make the same 200-mile trip in eight hours! There were no takers.

Source: *The Times of London; November 7, 1831; page 7, column 5.*

1836 Ernst walks from Constantinople to Calcutta and back in 59 days

Mensen Ernst grew up in the heart of Norway's fjord country. Though he earned his living as a sailor, he made his fame as a landlubber. He traversed Europe, Asia, and Africa on foot in unbelievable record time.

Little jaunts like a march from Paris to Moscow, or a hike from Germany to Greece, were nothing for this Norwegian. He took those kinds of walks in stride, so to speak.

In 1836, when he was 37 years old, the sturdy Viking took off from Constantinople (now Istanbul) and headed for Calcutta in eastern India. The two cities were 2,800 miles apart. The trip meant crossing mountains, rivers, badlands, and the deserts of the Middle East. Ernst trekked along for almost 100 miles each day; and when he reached Calcutta he hardly took time off for a nap, but did an about-face to return to Constantinople. He completed his two-way trip in 59 days, an over-all average of four miles an hour day and night, counting sleeping hours, too.

This was a 5,589-mile hike accomplished at a time when many roads were not paved, and through areas where in some localities there were no roads at all. No man has ever equaled this walking achievement.

Source: "Norsk Allkunnebok" (Encyclopedia of Norway); Fonna Forlag; 1948; volume 4, page 32.

1868 Holua surf rides a 50-foot wave

The sport of surfing originated many years ago in Hawaii. And appropriately enough, the most daring surfing feat ever recorded took place there. However, the feat was performed not for sport or recreational purposes, but in a struggle between life and death.

It happened on April 2, 1868, when the Kau area, in the southeastern part of the island of Hawaii, was suddenly battered by a destructive series of giant tidal waves. When the first wave struck, a man named Holua was working in his field at some distance from the coast. Hoping to save some money he had left in his house which was located in the seaside village of Ninole, he rushed home. One of the gigantic waves thundered in and lifted up the house while Holua was still inside. The wave carried Holua's home several hundred yards inland, then, as the wave receded, it swept the house out to sea.

Holua, a resourceful man, was also one of the most powerful swimmers in the district. When the house began to break up, he ripped loose a plank. Using it as a makeshift surfboard, he rode in on the next incoming wave, landing safely on the beach at Punaluu.

According to Holua's account, and the testimony of numerous witnesses on shore, the tidal wave he rode in on measured about 50 feet in height. His feat is seen to be all the more remarkable when one considers that most present-day surfing experts hold that waves more than 35 feet high are not ridable.

Source: Information provided by Mary M. Lee from library files of Bernice P. Bishop Museum, Honolulu. "Hawaiian Surfboard"; Tom Blake; Paradise of the Pacific Press; 1935; p. 57.

1882 Saunders runs 120 miles in less than 24 hours

One of the most unusual competitions that ever
took place was the track race held in the American
Institute's indoor arena in New York City on February 21,
1882, under the auspices of the Williamsburg Athletic Club.
The rules stipulated that the race would be 24 hours long.
The athlete who did the most mileage around the track in
that time would be declared the winner.

At 10:00 p.m., 14 competitors lined up for the race. After
23 hours had elapsed, only seven remained on the track.
James Saunders was so far ahead it seemed impossible for
anyone to beat him.

By common consent, the race was halted a few minutes
later—almost an hour before the stipulated finish. At this
point, Saunders had run 120 miles. He had won $100 in
cash, and the cheers of a crowd of 800 fans.

Source: *New York Herald; February 23, 1882; page 9, column 5.*

1884 Stevens rides around the world on a bicycle

The most ambitious cycling venture ever attempted by man was undertaken by Thomas Stevens in 1884. The young San Franciscan had decided to ride around the world on a bicycle.

Stevens was up against a few obstacles from the very start. For one thing, he didn't know how to ride a bike. But a little matter like that didn't seem to bother him. After just a few days of practice, Tom was off.

Stevens left San Francisco in April. In August, pedaling over more than 3,000 miles of rough roads and trails, he reached Boston. There he ran into another obstacle: he was broke. After a few months' delay, Colonel A. A. Pope, a prominent manufacturer of bicycles, agreed to back the adventurer, and Stevens sailed for Europe.

The tour through Europe on a bike was quite enjoyable. The sights were interesting, the roads were good; and when his giant 5-foot front wheel broke down, there was no lack of mechanics who could put the bike back in shape. By early 1884, thousands of Americans were following Stevens' adventure through newspaper accounts.

As Stevens traveled through Persia, India, and the Far East, the trip became more onerous. He was loaded down with gifts from Persian potentates and enthusiastic Chinese villagers. Usually, it took some time before the natives understood what Stevens was actually trying to accomplish, for the only language the American could speak was English.

Mile after mile the tireless Stevens pedaled on. Since,

on occasion, he had to struggle against pranksters and against animals who blocked his path on the roads, he refused to make time a factor. On some days he just didn't ride at all; on other days, he moved only by daylight.

But in January of 1887—less than three years after he had left home — Stevens returned, bicycle and all, to San Francisco. He was now famous, and his fame yielded him a considerable income through lectures and writings.

Source: "Annals of American Sport"; John Allen Krout; Yale University Press; 1929; page 175.

1885 Blondin crosses over Niagara Falls on a tightrope while pushing a wheelbarrow

P. T. Barnum, the great circus promoter, was never one to tell the truth if exaggeration might help to build a bigger gate. But the great P. T. never spoke truer words than on that day in 1855 when he introduced a 31-year-old Frenchman to the United States as "The World's Greatest Rope Walker."

Jean Francois Grandet, who used the name of Blondin because of his flowing blonde hair, was the daredevil supreme. No one before or since ever attempted stunts of such dramatic daring. He had a three-inch rope strung 1,100 feet across Niagara Falls. Balancing himself with a 40-foot pole, the intrepid Frenchman pedaled over the Falls on a bicycle. Scorning death, he once walked over the tightrope blindfolded. On another day, he pushed a wheelbarrow across the Falls on the tightrope.

On one occasion, he announced he was going to carry a man across the chasm piggy-back style. One hundred

thousand curious Americans and Canadians came to Niagara to see that one. The only one he could get to do the stunt with him was his manager.

On September 8, 1860, the Prince of Wales, who was touring North America, showed up in Canada to watch Blondin's final performance over the Falls. And what a show Blondin gave him!

Blondin attached short stilts to his legs; on each stilt, there was a hook which went around the rope. Halfway across the gorge, Blondin swung by the hooks head-down from the rope. Scores of men and women fainted, believing that he had lost his balance, fallen, and was going to plunge to his death. But Blondin had planned it all as a show-stopper. Hanging by the hooks, he swung gaily in his perilous position, and then nonchalantly got up and continued on to the Canadian shore.

The young prince, who was quite unnerved by the spectacle, said "Thank God, it's over. Please, never do it again." Blondin smiled and offered to give the prince a piggy-back ride across the rope. Scotland Yard escorts didn't think that remark was so funny, and they ushered the prince away.

Blondin went on to perform in Europe. The incredible man died in his bed at age 72.

Source: "Daredevils of Niagara"; Andy O'Brien; The Ryerson Press; Toronto; 1964; pages 82-83.

1891   Cyr outpulls four workhorses

He stood only five feet, ten and one half inches, but his huge chest, which bulged 60 inches in circumference, seemed like a barrel that had popped out of his 300-pound frame. His legs and his biceps were tremendous. So when he was billed as "The Strongest Man in the World," he looked the part.

The strength of the farm boy from St. Cyprein, Quebec, is the stuff that legends are made of. But Louis Cyr was no legend. He actually could lift a full barrel of cement with one arm, and he once pushed a freight car on the railroad tracks up an incline. On another occasion 18 men who in the aggregate weighed 4,300 pounds stood on a platform. Louis Cyr lifted the platform. And to get tongues wagging, Cyr lifted 588 pounds off the floor—with one finger!

But undoubtedly Cyr's most dramatic feat occurred on the day he was pitted against four workhorses. On December 20, 1891, standing before a crowd of 10,000, in Sohmer Park, Montreal, Louis Cyr was fitted with a special harness. Four draft horses were lined up opposite Cyr, a pair of them to his left, and a second pair to his right. Heavy leather straps encased his upper arms; sturdy hooks at the end of these straps were attached to whiffletrees which led to four harnesses strapped to four horses.

Cyr stood with his feet planted wide and placed his arms on his chest. As Louis gave the word the grooms urged their horses to pull. The regulations of the contest ruled out any sudden jerk. The four horses pulled with all their might and main on the strong man, trying to dislodge Louis' arms from his chest. If Cyr lost his footing or either arm left his chest, he would lose the contest.

The grooms whipped the horses, and urged them in every way to pull harder and harder. But the horses

slipped and slid, while Cyr didn't budge an inch. After
a few minutes of tugging, it was obvious that the victor
was stronger than all four horses put together.

Source: "The Strongest Man That Ever Lived"; George F. Jowett; Milo Publishing
Co.; 1927.

1892 Bogardus shoots 1,000 glass balls in 102 minutes

In the late 1800's, American shooting contests drew crowds of as high as 100,000. Captain A. H. Bogardus, New York born, moved to the Midwest in 1856. The lad found his new home to be great bird country, and he soon learned that a youngster could make a name for himself if he was considered to be the best shot around. Within the next dozen years, Bogardus became the finest trap shooter the Midwest had ever known.

As the nation's bird supply diminished, shooters turned to clay pigeons, and later to glass balls. In the early 1890's, when Bogardus was at his peak, the marksman put on a memorable performance before a record crowd in New

York's Gilmore Garden. While timers kept the score, Bogardus started shooting away at glass balls which were catapulted about 30 feet or so into the air. He shoved shells quickly into his breechloader, and ping! ping! ping! he banged down the balls one after another at record speed. He missed very few.

As Bogardus popped his 1,000th target, the official timer stopped his watch. The man had been shooting but one hour and 42 minutes, and had hit his targets on the average of 10 a minute. For almost two hours steady, Borgardus hit a glass ball every six seconds!

Source: "Annals of American Sport"; John Allen Krout; Yale University Press; 1929; pages 167-68.

1896 Harbo and Samuelson cross the Atlantic in a rowboat

In 1894, George Samuelson came up with an idea he thought might make him rich. If he could cross the Atlantic in a rowboat, people throughout Europe would pay him a fortune to see his craft and to hear him tell just how he did it.

For this strange adventure, Samuelson needed a partner. He approached a fellow seaman, one Frank Harbo, and convinced his countryman that it could be done. The fact that neither sailor had any experience rowing over a long distance didn't seem to deter these two Norwegians. A couple of years of practice would take care of that.

On June 6, 1896, Samuelson, now 26, and Harbo, now 30, left from New York harbor. Hundreds of people gathered to watch them take off. The New York Herald reported, "Seafaring men say it's nothing short of suicide."

Surprisingly, the novice adventurers had planned well. They built a sturdy rowboat from oak planks and cedar which was 18 feet, four inches long, and five feet wide. The two sailors loaded their craft down with 60 gallons of water, a supply of canned goods, oatmeal, and with five extra sets of oars. The supplies were so heavy that the boat sank until just 12 inches of plank bobbed above the water. For protection against violent weather, a canvas apparatus could be hoisted.

And so Harbo and Samuelson, choosing a route just south of that generally plied by steamships, steered for Le Havre, France, 3,250 miles away from New York. Each man put in

18 hours a day at the oars. Five hours a day were allowed for rest, and one hour a day for eating. They generally rested during the daytime, preferring to do their hard labor during the cool hours of the night. They had planned a schedule of 54 miles a day, and they kept to it.

About five weeks later, they passed a Norwegian freighter, which gave the two seafarers some fresh food and sped them on their way. Eleven days later, another freighter took the men on board for a short respite.

At this time, the rowing mariners decided they would do better if they headed for England. And so they did, shortening their trip by about 200 miles.

On August 1, 56 days after leaving New York, Harbo and Samuelson rowed onto a quiet coast of England. There were no cheering throngs to greet them as they completed one of the most daring voyages ever undertaken by man.

Source: New York Herald; August 2, 1896; Section 1, page 9, column 5.

1897 Bothner wins three different fencing titles in one year

Able to handle the foil, the épée, and the saber with equal grace, Charles Bothner won 10 American fencing titles during his heydey.

Mastering three blades is difficult. With the foil, which is similar to the short dress sword, only the trunk of the opponent's body is a valid target. With the heavier épée, any body touch counts. With the slashing saber, the touch can be made anywhere except on the legs, and any part of the blade can be used.

In 1897, wielding all three weapons with equal finesse, the mustachioed New Yorker won all three American titles.

Source: *"The Encyclopedia of Sports"; Frank G. Menke; A. S. Barnes; 1963; pages 333-34.*

1900 Houdini extricates himself from a straitjacket while hanging upside down in mid-air

During the early 1900's, the name of Harry Houdini was on everyone's lips, for this incomparable magician actually made newspaper headlines.

His repertoire of escape acts fascinated millions all over the world. So uncanny were his performances that many believed Houdini possessed supernatural powers. For even though Houdini vociferously denied being gifted with anything more than human attributes, his performances were so baffling that even his stout denials failed to squelch the talk. No one could fathom just how his stunts were accomplished; and it was not until after his death that his notebooks revealed how he contrived to do things which seemed beyond the powers of mortals.

One of his favorite stunts was to have himself bound by the police in a straitjacket used for the violently insane. No one, the police averred, could break out of this. But, in addition to the straitjacket, Harry had the police load him with iron shackles and ropes. Houdini was then upturned head down, and then hauled aloft in mid-air by means of a block and pulley. Then in full sight of an astounded audience and an absolutely dumbfounded police detail, the incredible man would wriggle free while upside down in mid-air. How did he do it?

Houdini was one of the greatest athletes that ever lived. From his early youth on, he had practiced body control. He could flex virtually every muscle in his body. His fingers had the strength of pliers; and his teeth were so strong that

they could be used like a can opener. His strength was so great that he could bend iron bars, and his tactile sensibility so fantastic that while blindfolded he could tell the exact number of toothpicks he was kneeling on.

Still, how did Houdini get out of that straitjacket? Answer: he contracted his muscles in such a way that he could slip one hand out of its bonds. By similar contractions and maneuverings, he would set his limbs free. Then the great locksmith would free himself from his iron fetters.

Houdini left explicit directions as to just how the stunt could be accomplished, but so far no athlete has come along with enough physical dexterity to perform the feat.

Source: "Houdini's Fabulous Magic"; Walter B. Gibson and Morris N. Young; Chilton Company; 1961; pages 39-42.

1900 Fitzsimmons KO's a man 140 pounds heavier than himself

On April 30, 1900, in Brooklyn, New York, Robert Fitzsimmons, a 37-year-old Englishman, fought Ed Dunkhorst, an American heavyweight. "Ruby Robert," as he was known, stood five feet 11¾ inches in height, and didn't look particularly robust at 165 pounds. Dunkhorst tipped the scales at a hearty 305.

Fitzsimmons' strategy was clear. He would move in with a flurry of punches and then back off from his opponent, move in again and then back off. He intended to wear Dunkhorst down.

In the second round, Ruby Robert dropped the big, hulking Dunkhorst to the floor, and Ed never got up to continue the battle. Fitzsimmons had beaten a man who outweighed him by 140 pounds!

During his career, Ruby Robert, one of the great fistic names of all time, held the championship in the middle-weight class, the light-heavyweight class, and the heavyweight class.

Source: "Ring Record Book"; Nat Fleischer; Ring Book Shop; 1967; page 743.

1900 Yielding walks on stilts 22 feet high

He grew up in Great Yarmouth, England, among a family of circus performers, and he grew up dabbling in all sorts of circus stunts. After years of practice, Harry Yielding became expert on those awkward high-rise contraptions called stilts.

During the early 1900's, Yielding performed dressed as a clown, and how the crowd did roar when they saw him walking along on stilts 22 feet high—just about two stories above the ground.

Source: "English Circus"; Ruth Manning-Sanders; Werner Laurie; 1952; page 283.

1900 Stewart and Oliver battle on a log for three hours and 15 minutes

The men in early American logging camps worked hard.
And they played hard, too. Their favorite contest was log
rolling, a sport which dates back to Revolutionary days.
Two men would stand on a round log which floated in
midstream. They would spin and twist the wood in different
directions until one lost his balance and fell off. It was
illegal to touch one's opponent.

The greatest log-rolling battle ever staged took place in 1900 in Ashland, Wisconsin. Two lumberjacks, Alan Stewart and Joe Oliver, were locked in a contest on a local river that went well beyond the few minutes that such battles usually lasted. Before Stewart sent his exhausted opponent for a spill, the two had been at it for three hours and 15 minutes.

Source: Wisconsin Historical Society; Madison, Wisconsin.

1901 Annie Taylor goes over Niagara Falls in a barrel

She was a childless, widowed, 43-year-old schoolteacher from Bay City, Michigan, and for the task at hand, her credentials were rather bland. For a first-time adventurer, her stakes were high.

On October 24, 1901, she would go over the 160-foot-high Horseshoe Falls in a barrel. Where others had failed, Annie Edson Taylor was willing to gamble. As it was, her life was going nowhere; if she succeeded, fame and fortune would follow.

On that big day, she made her entrance in a long black dress and fluttering hat. Only just before getting into her barrel would she change into a short skirt. For one thing she was prudish; for another, she weighed 160 pounds.

At Grass Island, Annie was lowered into the oak cask. From there, a rowboat took her out to where the currents would carry her to the falls. Of course, it was no ordinary barrel. Bound by seven iron hoops, it was four and one-half feet high, four feet in diameter, and it weighed 160 pounds. A hundred pound anvil was tied to its bottom as an anchor, to keep the barrel upright when it floated.

The cheering throngs that gathered along the Niagara gave Annie the attention she craved. "Au revoir," she told them majestically, as she was turned loose. "I'll not say goodbye because I'm coming back."

As the barrel was picked up by the strong current, the throng fell silent and wondered.

The barrel bobbed and flipped, and then it splashed over the break. For Annie, strapped inside, there could be no strategy other than to use her strong muscles to brace herself. Luckily, when the barrel hit bottom, it bounced away from the Falls, and her aides fished her out. It wasn't until later that they learned she couldn't swim!

For Annie, there was immediate fame; but sadly, no fortune. Brokenhearted, she again became an unknown, but never again an adventurer.

Source: "The Daredevils of Niagara"; Andy O'Brien; The Ryerson Press; 1964; pages 2-12.

1908 Ewry wins his tenth Olympic gold medal

When he was a child growing up in Lafayette, Indiana, Ray Ewry's legs were as wobbly as spaghetti: a case of polio had weakened his limbs. Ray's physician suggested that the lad strengthen his legs through constant jumping exercises.

Ewry followed this advice—and he did so, so perseveringly and so unstintingly, that he actually developed what were perhaps the strongest set of legs in history. In the 1890s;

Ewry went to Purdue University where he captained the track team. After he graduated, Ewry earned a place on the United States Olympic team. He was then 26 years old.

On July 16, 1900, in Paris, Ewry won three Olympic gold medals: the standing long jump, the standing high jump, and the standing hop, step and jump—all of which required a stationary start. In the standing high jump Ewry cleared 5 feet, 5 inches, nearly six inches better than his closest competitor.

In the 1904 Olympics, the lanky 6-foot, 3-inch athlete repeated his masterful performance. In 1906 (when a special Olympics was held), and in 1908, Ewry collected medals again for the standing long and high jumps. During a nine-year span, Ray collected 10 Olympic gold medals—no mean accomplishment when it is considered that no athlete, before or since, has won more than seven firsts in Olympic track and field events.

Source: "An Illustrated History of the Olympics"; Richard Schaap; Alfred A. Knopf; 1963; pages 59-60.

1912   Thorpe proves a champion in 11 sports

At the closing ceremony of the 1912 Olympic games in Stockholm, the King of Sweden singled out a youthful American Indian and said: "Sir, you are the greatest athlete in the world." Jim Thorpe was.

The young man from Carlisle Institute excelled in boxing, wrestling, lacrosse, gymnastics, swimming, hockey, handball, basketball, football, track, and baseball.

Indeed, many authorities rate Thorpe as the finest football player who ever lived. Playing for his college, Jim scored 25 touchdowns and 198 points in a single season. He could placekick 40 yards, and he could punt 80. He weighed but 190, but Thorpe was so tough that he once put four men who tried to tackle him out of the game. At 32, Thorpe got into professional football, and played so well he was named to pro football's Hall of Fame. At 42, Jim was still playing pro ball.

Jim played Major League baseball, too. He was still playing Minor League baseball at 41.

Thorpe was also a great track star. Once, in a dual collegiate meet, Thorpe scored enough points by himself to defeat the entire 47-man opposition. In the 1912 Olympics, Jim won both the pentathlon and the decathlon!

In 1953, the Associated Press polled its members to select the greatest male athlete of the half-century (1900-1950). Jim Thorpe drew more first-place votes than all the other nominees combined.

Source: "Britannica Book of the Year"; Encyclopedia Britannica; 1954; page 537.

1913 Edgerton wins a professional fight at age 63

When ex-boxer Walter Edgerton, age 63, challenged ex-boxer John Henry Johnson to a fight, Edgerton was at an age when most men would prefer to be puttering in their gardens.

Johnson was no kid, either — he was 45.

Back in the 1880's Edgerton had been a well-known featherweight — "Kentucky Rosebud" by name. But this was February, 1913, and his fighting days should have been long behind him.

One fine day at a bar, Edgerton got into an argument with another ex-boxer. Herman Taylor, a young promoter, heard about the quarrel and understood that the two wanted to settle their falling out with their fists. The age factor didn't faze them at all. So Taylor suggested they go into the ring at the Broadway AC. Not only would they end their altercation in the time-honored manner, but they would pick up some prize money as well.

And they did. The night Edgerton and Johnson squared off, the little AC was packed to its 800 capacity.

When he entered the ring at Philadelphia's Broadway Athletic Club, Edgerton didn't show an overabundance of push and go. At the start, it wasn't the fastest-moving bout on record. But Edgerton was conserving his strength. Before the fourth round was over, the young John Henry, Edgerton's junior by 18 years, was laid out like a plank, felled by the "Rosebud's" knockout punch.

Source: "Ring Record Book"; Nat Fleischer; Ring Book Shop; 1966 edition; page 743.

1913 Bliss drives a golf ball 445 yards

There is hardly a measurable record in sports that is
not erased by time. Men grow bigger and stronger; the
equipment constantly improves, and the techniques are
constantly refined—and in some sports—even revolutionized.
But in golf, a sport that during the last decade has seen the
emergence of such long-ball hitting professionals as
Jack Nicklaus and George Bayer, one record, surprisingly
enough, has held up for better than half a century.

Playing on the Old Course at Herne Bay, Kent, England,
during August of 1913, Edward Bliss, a 50-year-old
Englishman with a 12 handicap, put all of his 182 pounds
behind his swing and clubbed his ball of destiny. It zoomed
off for 445 yards, and made Bliss immortal in the world of
golf. Of course, the length of his shot included the bounces
and the roll, plus a 57-foot drop over the quarter mile trip.

On that particular day, Bliss was blessed with luck as
well as talent, for it so happened that a registered surveyor
happened to be on the course and took an accurate
measurement of the shot.

In the 1933 British Open, Craig Wood, an American star,
powdered the ball for 430 yards; and in the 1950's,
George Bayer, a hulking six-foot-five Canadian, knocked
one for a distance of 426. Jack Nicklaus, the 210-pound
professional, is credited by the Professional Golfers
Association with a record drive of 341 yards. Unofficially,
it is claimed that "Ohio Fats" has knocked the ball

considerably farther. But despite these onslaughts, Bliss'
mighty wallop of 1913 still holds up.

Source: "The Golfer's Handbook"; The Golfer's Handbook, Ltd.; 1967;
page 628.

1913 Brown beats six professional fighters on the same night

Most boxers prefer their fights just one at a time, with weeks of rest and training periods in between.

But consider the case of Preston Brown of Philadelphia's

Broadway Athletic Club. One night in 1913, he announced that he would take on all comers, and no fewer than six ring-wise professionals arose from the ranks.

Every one of the challengers was bigger than Brown. Nonetheless the plucky, 125-pound Negro took them on—

one by one—and he walloped them all. He knocked out five of the six—in early rounds, no less. The sixth challenger lost on a decision.

Source: Police Gazette Magazine; undated, 1913.
Letter from Harry Pegg, boxing historian; Philadelphia; May 22, 1968.

1913 Lewis chins the bar 78 consecutive times

Anton Lewis was a professional strong man. He traveled throughout the world giving exhibitions and shows.

In 1913, the Englishman, on stage before an audience in Brockton, Massachusetts, grabbed a high bar with both hands and hoisted his chin up alongside it. This in itself is an exercise common enough to be seen in any gymnasium. But Lewis' performance was extraordinary.

Generally speaking, a fairly good athlete can chin the bar between 10 and 16 times; chinning two dozen times is a standout performance. Before Lewis stopped that night in April, he had chinned the bar 78 times — a world's record that still holds!

Source: Strength & Health Magazine; October, 1937; page 18.

1915 Young runs a mile in 8:30 with a man on his back

In 1915, the world's record for the mile run was four minutes 14.4 seconds. On April 12th of that year, Noah Young, an Australian, ran around a Melbourne

track for the length of a mile in eight minutes 30 seconds, and established a world's record. How come?

Well, Young was carrying a man on his back. The runner weighed 198 pounds. The lad he was lugging along weighed 150. It was quite a performance.

Source: Melbourne (Australia) Herald; April 13, 1915; page 6, column 2.

1918 Wickham makes the greatest high dive in history

On March 23, 1918, Alick Wickham executed the highest
dive ever attempted, jumping from a platform atop
a cliff which bordered the Yarra River near Melbourne,
Australia, into a stream, the surface of which was allegedly
200 feet from the top of the platform.

Alick was born in the Solomon Islands of an English
father and a Polynesian mother. When the stunt was
announced, hordes of Australians came to watch him and
excitement was high. Bookmakers were laying odds of
five to one that he wouldn't even try it; some even offered
odds of 10 to one that Wickham wouldn't survive if he did try
it. But if Wickham lacked prudence, he certainly had an
abundance of raw courage.

Starting in a swan dive, half-way down Wickham lost
consciousness. He hit the surface of the water with
so powerful an impact that his bathing suit was ripped right
off his body. When he bobbed up above the water line, he
signaled for a blanket and then made it safely to shore.
But the stunt took its toll, for he suffered internal injuries and
was laid up for three weeks.

There is some question about the exact height of the
dive. The Melbourne Herald reported the distance as
"200 feet or thereabouts." The Australian Encyclopaedia
claimed that the dive was made from a height of 205 feet;
while the Melbourne Argus stated that "The height
of the platform appeared to be anything between 100 feet
and 150 feet, but officially it was claimed to be over

200 feet." Apparently there is no clear indication in these reports just how high the cliff was and how high the platform was. However, all observers seem to have been agreed that the total height was over 200 feet, or a height exceeding 20 stories of an office building.

Source: Melbourne Herald; March 23, 1918. Melbourne Argus; March 25, 1918. Australian Encyclopaedia; page 382.

1918   Moir drives in 1,409 rivets in one hour

During World War I, the German U-boat campaign
took a heavy toll of British shipping. In order to preserve its
lifeline of supplies, England was compelled to step up its
shipbuilding activity. To encourage production and to render
routine jobs more interesting and more honorific, the
British set up competitions in their shipyards.

In a riveting contest held in the yards of the Workman &
Clark Co., one John Moir, who hailed from Belfast, put on a
performance which laid all existing records to rest.
On a June day of 1918, Moir drove 1,409 ⅞-inch metal
rivets into the floor of a ship in one hour's time, ramming
in the pegs at an average of better than 23 per minute.
During the full nine-hour work day, the Irishman banged
in a total of 11,209 rivets, an average of 1,245 rivets per
hour. Moir hardly took time off to eat or drink, as he
achieved his record performance of one rivet every three
seconds for a full nine-hour span!

Source: The Times of London; June 14, 1918; page 2, column 4.

1918   Lillian Leitzel chins the bar 27 times with one hand

By profession, Lillian Leitzel was an aerialist. She had performed in a number of circuses, including the famous Ringling Brothers and Barnum & Bailey production. This pint-sized acrobat—only 4 feet, 9 inches tall and weighing 95 pounds—was gifted with a strength that was almost unbelievable.

The record for one-handed chin-ups by a male athlete at the time was held by an Englishman named Cutler, who in 1878 completed 12 one-handed chin-ups. The difficulty of chinning with one hand is well recognized.

So when Lillian came to Hermann's Gym in Philadelphia in 1918 to work out with some acrobats, the gymnasts who were present scoffed at her claim that she could best the world's record for one-handed chin-ups. Lillian was 36 years old at the time.

Responding to the offer of a small, friendly wager to test her boast, Miss Leitzel took to the bar and clicked off 27 right-armed chin-ups in a row. After the pay-off and a short rest, Lillian had one more shock left for the bystanders. She leaped to the bar—this time with her LEFT hand!—and did 19 more one-handed chin-ups—a performance that again broke the male right-hand record.

Source: "Center Ring"; Robert Lewis Taylor; Doubleday; 1956; page 222.

1918   Oliphant wins his 24th college letter

Winning a college letter is a mark of achievement in sports. To win letters in more than one sport is the mark of versatility.

As a teenager, Elmer Oliphant had toughened and honed his 175-pound body in the coal mines of southern Indiana. At Purdue University, he became a star in football, earning All-Conference honors in each of his three seasons on the varsity. In baseball, Oliphant caught behind the bat, and also played the outfield. To round it all out, he also played basketball and ran in track meets. Before he left Purdue, Elmer had accumulated 12 varisity letters.

He then entered the United States Military Academy at West Point where, due to the war, he was permitted to participate in intercollegiate competition, even though he was a graduate of another school. So as a military cadet, Oliphant played varsity football for four years more, and earned four more letters. Which to the three he gained at the Point in baseball, and the three in basketball, the one in track, and still another in hockey, added up to an even dozen merit badges, bringing his total to 24.

Just for good measure, Elmer Oliphant made the West Point swimming team, and won the annual West Point heavyweight boxing championship.

Source: "The Big Ten"; Kenneth L. (Tug) Wilson and Jerry Bronfield; Prentice-Hall, Inc.; 1967; page 81.

1920 Malone scores seven goals in one professional hockey game

When the National Hockey League came into being in 1917, the 27-year-old Joe Malone of Quebec City was already a hockey veteran. By this time, he had been scampering over the ice professionally for 10 years.

In the 1920 Stanley Cup series, playing for the Quebec Bulldogs on January 31st, Joe matched goal for goal with the whole Toronto team. First, the opposing team would score a goal, and then Malone would match it. The seesaw struggle went on all night. When the fracas was over, Toronto had scored six goals, but Malone, all by himself, had scored seven. Quebec won the game by a score of 10 to 6.

It's nearly half a century since Malone's performance, and nobody has as yet broken Malone's record. It's a good bet that nobody ever will.

Source: The National Hockey League Guide; 1967; page 36.

1920 Swahn competes in the Olympic games at age 73

As an accountant employed in the Stockholm office of the Swedish Telegram Bureau, Oscar G. Swahn must have seemed an ordinary enough person, but he was one of the

finest riflemen who ever lived. During his 65-year career, he won more than 500 awards and prizes and he was a member of the Swedish shooting team at four meetings of the Olympic Games. His specialty was the running-deer event.

At the Paris Games in 1900, Swahn won a gold medal in the single-shot running-deer event. In 1908, at the London Games—where at age 61 he was the oldest participant in any event—Swahn again won a gold medal in the single-shot running-deer, a bronze medal in the double-shot, and helped win a gold medal for Sweden in the team single-shot event.

The 1912 Games were held in Stockholm, Swahn's home town. Competing before the admiring eyes of thousands of his countrymen, Swahn, again the oldest competitor, was a member of the gold-medal team in the single-shot running-deer event, and the bronze-medal team in the double-shot.

Because of World War I, the Olympic Games were not held in 1916. But at the first peacetime session of the Games, held in Antwerp in 1920, Swahn competed at the amazing age of 73. He helped win a team silver medal for Sweden in the single-shot, and a team bronze in the double-shot.

Four years later, Swahn once more qualified for the Swedish shooting team. At the last minute, though, he was prevented by illness from participating in the Games. He died in 1927 at the age of 80.

Source: "Nordic Family Books Sports Encyclopedia"; translation provided by Swedish Information Service, New York City.

1920 Rastelli juggles 10 balls

Enrico Rastelli was one of the greatest jugglers and acrobats of all time. A magnificently coordinated athlete, he had the highest paid novelty act of any kind when he worked the Keith-Albee-Orpheum vaudeville circuit in the United States in the 1920s.

The son and grandson of performers, Rastelli was born in 1896 in Samara, Russia, where his parents were on tour with the famous Circus Truzzi. He learned juggling from his father, and at the age of 12, he displayed his budding talent by doing a handstand on his father's head while juggling four lit torches.

The wiry 5-foot 6-inch Rastelli soon gained fame for many incredible feats. He would do a handstand on a lamp which stood on a table, while he was also holding an 8-foot flagpole (which flew the Italian flag) with one foot, and juggling two balls with his other foot. Rastelli could also jugggle six 24-inch sticks while keeping a seventh stick balanced on his head, and he could juggle eight plates at one time.

However, his most famous stunt was the one in which he flashed ten balls at one time—that is, simultaneously kept five balls constantly moving with each hand. No juggler since has been able to duplicate this feat.

Source: Bill Gnadt, International Jugglers' Association.

1923 Tangora types 147 words per minute for one hour straight

On October 23, 1923, Albert Tangora of Paterson, New Jersey, typed an average of 147 words a minute for one full hour, a record that has not been surpassed in the succeeding half-century. Tangora's performance took place in a competition at the 20th Annual Business Show, held at New York City's 69th Regiment Armory.

In one hour of non-stop typing, Tangora ran off a total of 8,840 words (inclusive of a 10-word-per-error penalty)—a rate of 147 words a minute. The judges estimated that Tangora executed an average of 12-1/2 strokes per second.

After a brief rest, Tangora returned to his machine to win a 60-second sprint, typing 150 words within the single minute without making an error.

Source: New York Times; October 23, 1923; page 5, column 1.

1924 Nurmi wins two Olympic distance races in one day

On July 10, 1924, in the games held in Paris, Paavo Nurmi was entered in two Olympic finals. The Finn would run in the 1,500 meters, and also in the 5,000 meters; and the two events were scheduled but 50 minutes apart.

Not only did Paavo win both races, but he established two Olympic records in the process.

The 1,500 came first. At 100 meters, Nurmi took the lead. Shortly thereafter, he stretched his margin to 10 yards. Then with a lap to go, the Finnish speedster peered at his stopwatch, liked what he saw, and tossed his watch off to the sidelines. Nurmi fans knew what that meant: their blond hero was on schedule and was ready to step up the pace. As he crossed the finish line in 3:53.6—only a second off his world record—he kept on running, right into the locker room. There, he nibbled on dried fish, and then took a brief rest.

A half hour later, Paavo Nurmi was back on the track again for the 5,000. For the first 3,000 meters, Nurmi maintained his pace, often referring to his stopwatch. Ritola, another Finn, and an arch rival, stayed close at Willie's heels.

Then Ritola burst into the lead. Thirty thousand throats at Colombes Stadium broke into a roar as the two Finns battled step for step. Then Nurmi looked at his watch again, decided he had had enough of this parrying, discarded his timepiece, and broke into a sprint. About 20 yards from the finish, Nurmi turned his head and saw Ritola nearly abreast of him. Then Paavo put on a final burst, and won by a yard. His time was 14:31.2.

Nurmi's finish was so tremendous that Grantland Rice, dean of American sportswriters, ecstatically reported, "The superman has arrived at last!"

Source: *Chicago Tribune; July 10, 1924; page 1, column 3.*

1924 Peters kicks 17 field goals in one football game

On November 1, 1924, Montana State University's freshman football team was pitted against Billings Polytech. In that game, one Forest Peters attempted 22 field goals. He made 17 of them.

Scoring 12 field goals through an entire season's play would mark anyone as a good kicker. Scoring 17 in a single game—well, history hath no parallel.

Source: "Football Facts and Figures"; Dr. L. H. Baker; Farrar & Rinehart; 1945; page 121-22.

1924 Plaisted wins a professional rowing race at age 74

When he was 17, Frederick Plaisted won his first professional rowing race, and with it $500 in cash. But it was his very last stakes race—a race that occurred 57 years later—that earned Plaisted immortality.

Fred was 74 years old when he and two old professional rivals, Jim Ten Eyck and Jim Riley, set up a match in Saratoga to determine who was the best of the three. Plaisted, then of Philadelphia, found a backer who put up $1,000 for him. (Plaisted was finicky about his backers, and for good reason. He once went to China to race for $10,000 cash, only to find after his victory that $10,000 cash in Chinese money was worth $10 in American specie.)

At 5 a.m. on that morning in 1924, the three lined up before a crowd of 1,000 onlookers. The course was marked off at three miles—a good-sized race for rowers of any age bracket. The betting was fairly heavy.

For the first half-mile all three rowers seemed surprisingly strong. Then Ten Eyck, the rowing coach at Syracuse, faded. Riley, who had the advantage of being on his own course, pressed on, staying within striking distance of Plaisted.

But Plaisted, once a 240-pounder who now weighed in at 185, had power to burn. By the halfway mark, Fred was away by himself. As Riley grew weaker at the finish, Plaisted came in with considerable margin to spare, in the impressive time of 21 minutes, 4 seconds.

Fred Plaisted never raced again for money, but he did

race again. He celebrated his 89th birthday by defeating
John B. Kelly, an ex-Olympic champion and a much younger
man, in a race on the Schuylkill in Philadelphia.

On his 91st birthday, Fred admitted to rowing three miles
every other day, just to keep in shape. When interviewed,
he said, "Technically, I am a better rower now than
I ever was." He died when he was 95.

Source: *Philadelphia Record; July 7, 1935.*
Associated Press "Biographical Sketch"; dated January 15, 1941.

1925 Suzanne Lenglen wins the tennis championship at Wimbledon

In the 1920's, the big name in women's tennis was Suzanne Lenglen. The French girl had won her first world's championship when she was in her mid-teens; from 1917 to 1926, the tennis queen had lost only one match and that happened when she was ill.

Suzanne always contrived to be spectacular during the championship matches at Wimbledon, the showplace of international tennis. She had won the singles here five years in a row, from 1919 to 1923, and she marked her virtuosity with an additional stamp by capturing the title in doubles during the same five years.

In 1924, the queen defaulted at Wimbledon and also withdrew from the 1924 Olympic championships. The tennis world was suspecting that perhaps Mademoiselle Lenglen feared that her reign had come to an end, and that she would be humbled by the upcoming young American star, Helen Wills.

However, in 1925, Suzanne entered the Wimbledon lists once again. She was going to stop the mouths of the gossipers; and indeed, she put on a show which no one will ever forget. In the two preliminary matches she simply overwhelmed her opponents 6-0, 6-0. That kind of thing was nothing new for La Lenglen, for there were only a handful of girls who belonged on the court with her anyway.

But when Suzanne roared through the quarterfinals and the semifinals and devastated her opponents with equally blistering 6-0, 6-0 scores, the stands stood up and took notice.

Matched in the finals against Joan Fry of England, Suzanne lost but two games in the first set, as she juggernauted to victory. Throughout the entire tournament, Lenglen had yielded but a brace of games, and had won every single set.

Source: "The Story of Tennis"; Lord Aberdare; Stanley Paul; 1959; page 190.
New York Times; July 4, 1925; page 8, column 1.

1926   Giola dances the Charleston continuously for 22½ hours

In the 1920's, the Charleston held young America in thrall. While enthusiasts danced to exhaustion, some of their elders considered the gyrations intemperate, and their outcry was sufficient to convince a number of colleges to ban the dance on campus. But bluenoses notwithstanding, the Charleston took over and became the craze of the day.

At midnight on February 2, 1926, 10 men and 18 women entered a Charleston contest under the auspices of Broadway's famed Roseland Dancing Academy. The idea was to see who could dance the Charleston longest.

Three and one-half hours after the start, two of the girls collapsed. A little while later, a man was carted off to the hospital in the pangs of exhaustion. At 7:45 a.m. the next day, the last female entrant dropped out: she had fainted.

But several men, now tieless, danced on. However, the ranks continued to thin. By noontime—twelve hours after the start—only four competitors remained on the floor. These four sipped coffee and nibbled sandwiches while violently moving in time with the furious beat of the band. By early evening, only three competitors remained aloft.

At 10:30 p.m. the performance took on a macabre aspect, and the manager of Roseland became concerned. The three men on the floor now looked more like pulsating corpses than dancers. Exactly 22 and one-half hours after the start, the show was stopped "for humane reasons."

The contest officials awarded the silver cup to the man whom they considered to be in the best condition, one John

Giola. This 23-year-old father of two had, just two weeks earlier, gone through four blood transfusions to aid a young child.

The award was popular with the audience, but one of the remaining finalists argued the decision. The third man didn't — he had collapsed.

Source: New York Herald Tribune; February 4, 1926; page 1, column 7.

1927 Sepalla averages 11 miles per hour by dog sled

For a quarter of a century, Leonhard Sepalla was considered to be the best dog-sled racer in Alaska. During his long career, he had possessed and trained 1,000 sled dogs, and he had made a name for himself in the frozen north by rushing the sick to hospitals and rushing medical supplies to the sick by dog sled over the trackless wastes.

In February of 1927, Sepalla, then aged 50, came down to the United States and entered the New England Point-to-Point race, which initiated in the town of North Conway, New Hampshire. It was to be a run of 133½ miles down to Wolfeboro, New Hampshire. Oldtimers who were supposed to know, predicted that Sepalla's little Siberian malamutes would never be able to hold up on the jagged,

icy trails and mountainous terrain of New England; it would take crossbred huskies to negotiate the steep inclines. But Sepalla thought otherwise.

In order to avoid congestion on the trail, the starting teams were staggered, departing on the race a few minutes apart. When the signal for him to leave was given, Sepalla pulled the green shade down over his eyes and began talking to his little Siberians. The man chattered to his dogs all the way, and one onlooker said that it seemed that Sepalla's constant talk lulled the dogs into a hypnotic state. But be that as it may, his faithful animals obeyed his every word.

As he checked into Wolfeboro, 2,000 fans found out what Alaskans had known for years: that Leonhard Sepalla was the best man who ever drove a dog sled over ice and snow. The champion had traversed more than 133 miles in a little over 12 hours, an average speed of better than 11 miles per hour.

Source: Associated Press dispatch; February 14, 1927.

1927 Sonja Henie wins the world's champion figure-skating title at age 13

Sonja Henie was given her first pair of ice skates when she was six—an old-fashioned model that she strapped onto her shoes. Just one year later, she won a skating competition, the first she ever entered. Her competitors were twice her age.

Two years later, at age nine, she became Norway's figure skating champion. According to the experts, little Sonja skated better than any other woman in the country.

In 1927, the premier skaters of the world were gathered in Frogner Stadium in Oslo for the world's figure skating championship. The judges declared that Sonja Henie, then thirteen, was the best figure skater in the world.

During the next three Olympics, Miss Henie reigned supreme. Her fame became world-wide and she went to the United States to star in the movies where she earned millions of dollars.

Source: "Wings on My Feet"; Sonja Henie; Prentice-Hall; 1940; page 23.

1928 Vanderstuyft rides a bike 76 miles in one hour

On October 1, 1928, Leon Vanderstuyft mounted his bike and began to spin around the famed Autodrome at Linas Montlhery, France. The Belgian racer, paced by a motorcycle, pedaled for one complete hour. When he was done, the officials measured his distance at 76 miles, 504 yards.

Even with the improved equipment of today, no one has ever endangered that mark.

Source: *The Times of London*, October 2, 1928; page 5, column 6.

1928 Wolf wins the American Bowling Congress title at age 60

When Phil Wolf, of Chicago, entered the American Bowling Congress tournament competition in 1928, he had an established reputation behind him. He had been competing in ABC national tournaments since 1905, when he was a young man of 37. Now Wolf entered the lists at the ripe age of 60.

Phil won.

Source: *Letter from Bowling Magazine; Milwaukee, Wisconsin; June 18, 1968.*

1929   Finn runs 100 yards in a sack in 14.4 seconds

Nowadays, sack races are usually held as entertainments during church outings or family picnics. But there was a time earlier in this century when the sack race was a regular event on many track and field schedules. The winner of such a contest scored just as many points for his team as did a pole vaulter or a miler.

The best sack racer ever was an Irish-American from Brooklyn, New York, by the name of Johnny Finn. On May 1, 1929, in New York's 106th Regiment Armory, Finn competed in the 100-yard race — the popular distance in sack events. Each of the contestants lined up at the starting line, each one standing up to his neck in a cumbersome burlap bag. The oddness of grown-up men enmeshed in a such a get-up brought the usual laughter from the crowd. However, with the crack of the starter's gun, everyone settled down to business. The athletes waddled, hopped, stumbled, and shuffled down the straightaway.

At the finish, it was Finn as usual who was home first, breaking the tape at 14.4 seconds for a world's record. Just how fast that was may be gathered from the fact that on that same night—in the same meet—the 100-yard dash was won by a sprinter who covered the distance in 10.4 seconds.

Source: Brooklyn Eagle; May 2, 1929; page A-7, column 3.

1929 Monteverde wins a footrace from New York to San Francisco at age 60

Anyone who saw the group of athletes line up at City Hall in New York City on May 6, 1929, for a footrace to San Francisco, might have wondered at the sight of a 60-year-old man among the group of youths seeking international athletic fame.

Looking at the oldster—seemingly so out of place—one might have chuckled. But for those competitors who knew of the exploits of Abraham Lincoln Monteverde, his presence was certainly no laughing matter. He was, indeed, a competitor to be reckoned with. The old boy had been running for years, and he had completed more than one hundred 26-mile, 365-yard marathons. Moreover, he had taken part in these grueling races even after he had turned fifty.

This race—New York to San Francisco—was going to be the longest footrace in recorded history. The route was 3,145 miles. The rules provided that one could either walk or run. The only condition was that the distance must be traveled on foot. The race was supervised by the Amateur Athletic Union. It would bring the contestants through the major cities of the country; the first stop, Philadelphia. As the grueling trek wore on, Monteverde's younger competitors dropped out one by one. The pace was too telling, and when the oldster neared San Francisco, he had no company at all. Everyone had quit.

Abraham Lincoln Monteverde reached the San Francisco

City Hall at 7:10 P.M. on July 24, 1929. He had marched across the country in 79 days, 10 hours, and 10 minutes.

Source: New York Times; July 26, 1929; page 17, column 8.
"The Encyclopedia of Sports"; Frank G. Menke; A. S. Barnes; 1963; page 914.

1930 Bradman scores 452 runs in a cricket game

He was born in 1908 and entered top competition in the game in 1927. From then on until he retired in 1949, Don Bradman was a standout. Most Englishmen are willing to admit that this Australian was the finest cricket player who ever lived. Just before his career ended, he was knighted by King George VI and is now known as Sir Donald Bradman.

In his initial game, Bradman scored 118 runs. From then on, he was the most prolific scorer the game has ever known. His exploits crowd the record books.

Undoubtedly, his finest moment came in 1930 when he established a record for runs in a first-class competition. In a game between New South Wales and Queensland, Bradman, playing for New South Wales, scored an incredible 452 runs. He had been at the crease for seven hours, scoring at a rate of over one run per minute.

During his brilliant career, Bradman averaged 99.94 runs per innings in international "test" matches and 95.14 runs per innings in first-class competition. Any player, then or now, with an average in the fifties, would rank among the best. Bradman can be compared to a baseball star who batted .500 during a long career.

Source: "A History of Cricket"; Volume 2; E. W. Swanton; George Allen and Unwin, Ltd.; 1962; pages 309-10.
World Sport; June, 1968; page 8.

1930 Jones wins the U.S. Open on a 40-foot putt

The year was 1930. Bobby Jones had won the championship of the British Isles. On his return to the U.S., Wall Street gave the young hero a ticker tape parade.

A short while later, the best in the country had gathered at Minneapolis' Interlachen Course to determine who was to be named U.S. Open champion. In the first round, Jones

shot a 71; in the second, a 73. But a disastrous series of misplays in the final round put Bobby into a tie as he came up to the 18th hole.

Now it was up to Jones to make his decision. Should he play the hole safe, go for a tie, and let the final outcome await a play-off? Or should he go for broke, shoot directly for the hole — and possibly blow the tournament?

Jones decided to go all out. His first two shots were good— exceptionally good. But though he reached the green in two, unfortunately his ball lay 40 feet from the cup. It looked like a near impossible putt.

Bobby stood over his putter, "Calamity Jane," took aim, and then stroked the ball firmly. The little white sphere seemed to follow a magic line, breaking neatly in the last six feet and dropping into the hole. The crowd went wild.

That summer, Jones won the U. S. Amateur, his fourth championship of the year. The man had scored a grand slam, winning every major tournament, an accomplishment that was to make him eternally famous in the annals of golf.

Source: "Golf Is My Game"; Robert Tyre (Bobby) Jones; Doubleday; 1960; pages 145-152.

1932 Kershalla scores 71 points in one football game

It was November 19, 1932. West Liberty State, of
West Virginia, was pitted against Cedarville College. On
the very first play of the game, it was obvious Joe Kershalla
was going to have a good day: the West Liberty halfback
raced 70 yards for a touchdown. Before the day was
over, Kershalla had made football history. He had scored
71 points all by himself—a collegiate record.

Six of Kershalla's touchdowns were scored in the first
half of the game, as West Liberty rolled up an 83-0 lead.
At game's end, the score was 127-0.

But the feat has a rather weird aspect, for no one knows
for sure whether Kershalla was or was not a bona fide
collegian. To this day, West Liberty State has no evidence
that Kershalla was ever duly enrolled. It is suspected that
he was a ringer, for the records show that he scored only
one touchdown in the first eight games of that year; and
the records indicate that Joe wasn't listed as a starter in
any game after the Cedarville blockbuster.

But if Joe Kershalla's 71 points stand in question, there's
another West Liberty man who surely did score 67 points
in one game. The feat of halfback Bob Campiglio is
beyond cavil.

Source: "Ronald Encyclopedia of Football"; Harold Claassen and Steve Boda, Jr.;
Ronald Press Co.; 1963; Chapter 3, page 1.
Letter from Art Barbeau, public relations staff, West Liberty State
College; April 23, 1968.

1932 Beatty enters an arena that contains 50 lions and tigers

The greatest animal trainer who ever lived was just 5 feet, 5 inches tall. Until his death in 1965, Clyde Beatty was considered to be without peer in the handling of wild beasts. He would enter a cage armed only with a .38-caliber pistol that could hardly kill a flea. His weapon was loaded only with blanks which he used at times simply to scare his charges.

During a long career, the curly-headed Midwesterner faced thousands and thousands of lions, tigers, leopards, bears, ocelots and jaguars. Of course, this exposure yielded its untoward results. Time and again, Beatty was clawed and he bore the scars from over 100 maulings by wild cats, some of which weighed over 500 pounds.

Beatty's routine called for him to spend about a quarter of an hour locked up in a cage with anywhere from 12 to 24 lions and tigers. But on one occasion, he undertook to handle

50 of the big cats. Nobody, either before or since, has ever essayed such a feat. But Beatty was really a master.

Holding a whip in one hand and a chair in the other, he kept all the animals in their places. Using the crack of his whip, low whispers, blank shots from his pistol, and even screams, he kept this full menagerie of roaring, snarling beasts under control.

The feat is all the more remarkable when it is realized that it is virtually impossible for a man to keep 50 caged lions and tigers within the range of his peripheral vision. Clyde solved this problem by keeping his chair tilted toward the direction where he wasn't looking, while the animals in the range of his glare felt the constant threat of being whipped. Whenever a lion threatened to lunge at Beatty, he froze stark still, stared the animal down, and held up his chair for protection. With his other hand, he threatened with his whip.

However, before the day was over, even the unusually game Clyde Beatty admitted that 50 animals on a rampage at one time would have been even too much for him to manage.

He never tried it again.

Source: "Facing the Big Cats"; Clyde Beatty with Edward Anthony; Doubleday; 1965. New York Times; July 20, 1965; page 33, column 3.

1933 Knox bowls a perfect game without seeing the pins

Bowling a perfect game, though admittedly rare, is not an unheard-of feat. Most every top professional has bowled a perfect game at one time or other during his career. But nobody has ever equaled the feat of Bill Knox, who in 1933 knocked down the tenpins 12 times in a row without ever seeing them.

Knox had a special screen built at the Olney Alleys of Philadelphia and instructed two pin boys to hold the

screen about one foot above the foul line. The screen would hide the pins from the sight of the bowler and would even block off the sight of the lane itself. But the fans sitting in the stands could see over the top of the screen. Knox's purpose was to show bowlers the effectiveness of "spot" bowling—choosing a point on which to lay down the ball.

His control was so unbelievable that the sphere was in the perfect groove 12 times out of 12. Bill Knox had bowled a perfect game without ever seeing the target.

Source: *Letter from Edward Marcou, Editor, Bowling Magazine; December 6, 1968.*

1934 Franks swings an Indian club 17,280 times an hour

On August 2, 1934, working out in a gymnasium in Newcastle, Australia, William Franks picked up a heavy club and began swinging it around his head at an amazing speed. It was the typical Indian club, shaped like a bowling pin, popularly used by gymnasts until the early 1950's.

But Franks wasn't just out for exercise. Twirling the club at a rate of about 300 times a minute, Franks kept up his performance for a full hour. When he was done, the scorekeepers and timekeepers had recorded 17,280 twirls of the wooden pin—a record for sure!

Source: Sydney Morning Herald; August 3, 1934; page 8, column 3.

1934 Nilsson crosses the United States on a unicycle

Walter Nilsson was a vaudeville performer who was touted on the stage as "The King of the Unicycles." In 1934, Nilsson proved that his star billing was entirely justified. In those days, Robert Ripley, creator of *Believe It or Not* books, was in great vogue. He actually ran an annual contest to encourage daredevils and weirdos to attempt strange feats. Nilsson decided to get into the act. Accompanied by a representative of the Ripley organization, Nilsson left New York with intent to travel, by unicycle, to California, a distance of 3,306 miles.

Poised on top of an 8½-foot high contraption, Walter began his strange trek. Though the ride was painful, and Nilsson developed physical ailments that would bother him for the rest of his life, never once did the 33-year-old actor fall off his bike. Some 117 days after he left New York, Nilsson pedaled into San Francisco to earn a hero's welcome and win Ripley's award as having pulled off "The Most Unbelievable Feat of the Year."

Source: *American Bicyclist; April, 1939.*
Santa Monica (California) Evening Outlook; December 26, 1957; section 2, page 1, column 1.

1935 Levitt makes 499 straight free throws

Four thousand basketball fans hied to the Madison Street Armory in Chicago on April 6, 1935, to witness various basketball contests held under the auspices of the Amateur Athletic Union. At 7:00 p.m. that night, Harold Levitt—"Bunny," as he was called—stood on the foul line and heaved foul shots into the basket. Before the clock struck midnight, Levitt had dunked 499 consecutive free throws with his underhanded, two-hands-on-the-ball pitch. He then missed on his 500th shot.

At this point the crowd was through but Levitt wasn't. He just stood at the same spot and threw in 371 more shots without a miss. It was now 2:30 in the morning, and since an impatient janitor wanted to close up, Levitt was obliged to stop.

Later, Bunny hooked up with the world-famous Harlem Globetrotters, who offered $1,000 to any man who could beat Levitt in a contest of 100 foul shots. The money was never claimed. The best any challenger ever scored was 86; the worst performance Levitt ever turned in was 96.

It becomes germane to ask why, if Levitt was such a matchless foul shooter, did he never achieve fame as either a college player or a basketball pro. The reason is simple: Bunny stands only five feet, four inches tall.

Source: Chicago Tribune; December 21, 1962; page 37, column 2.

1935 Grange ends football career with over 19 miles in rushing yardage

It is October the 18th, 1924. A crowd of 60,000 fans has assembled to witness the opening of the new Memorial Stadium at the University of Illinois. But the crowd is not too sanguine about the chances of the Illini, who are running up against a formidable Michigan team, a team which has not been defeated during the past four years.

The stands are hushed as Michigan kicks off. The ball makes a long parabola down the field, and falls into the waiting arms

of an unknown young man, who can be identified only as
No. 77. Harold Grange tucks the ball in his arms, fakes to the
right, and then speeds down the middle of the gridiron. The
Michigan team converges on him, but Grange miraculously
bursts between the first two men, pivots to the left, swerves to
the right, and then in a split second, as the crowd goes stark
wild, is clear in the open, and speeds downfield to a touchdown.
The run is 95 yards.

During the first 12 minutes of play, Grange ran up four
touchdowns in just four carries. Before the day was over, the
red-headed youngster had set the Michigan team on its ear. His
statistics for the day were five touchdowns on the ground,
one pass to a teammate for a score, plus an incredible
338 yards gained rushing.

The telegraph wires rang with his exploits. Some imaginative
scribbler endowed the young wonder with the moniker of
"The Galloping Ghost," and from that time on, that's what the
5-foot, 11-inch flash was known as throughout the length
and breadth of the United States.

For Grange turned out not to be a one-day wonder. Week after week, he continued to electrify the stands as he multiplied his exploits, and turned tricks rarely, if ever, seen before on the football field. The great sports columnist, Grantland Rice, apostrophized the 175-lb. redhead in the following words:

> A *streak of fire, a breath of flame,*
> *Eluding all who reach to clutch;*
> A *gray ghost thrown into the game*
> *That rival hands may never touch.*

Grange became an immediate legend.

He resided in Wheaton, Illinois. When in high school, he used to work on ice trucks during the summer, so one writer called him "The Wheaton Iceman." When that fact became known, hundreds of youngsters, believing that such labor was the sure path to stardom, applied for similar work. It seemed that there were more kids ready to carry ice than there were cakes of ice.

Perhaps the most wonderful thing about Grange is that he played football at all; for when he was a high school kid, he suffered a crushed leg. The doctor said he would never be able to take part in athletics again. But Grange wouldn't stick with the verdict. He spent hours and hours exercising his shattered muscles, strengthening his leg. Later, in one game, the lanky youngster scored six touchdowns and kicked seven field goals for a score of 57 points!

At the University of Illinois, Red was named All-American for three straight seasons.

Undoubtedly, Grange was the man who put professional football on the map. Before him, the pros didn't amount to a row of dried-out corn. But when it was announced that the Galloping Ghost was going to play, that attraction was enough to fill up the stands. During an era when the sport was as popular as the measles, crowds of 70,000 turned out to watch him play.

Grange was paid as much as $300,000 a season, and even got another $300,000 to play in a movie.

When, in 1935, Red Grange retired, his records indicated that in 247 games in high school, college, and professional play he had carried the ball 4,013 times for a total gain of 33,820 yards. This was an average of better than 8 yards per play—over 19 miles in toto. No one ever has come close to this record.

Source: The Readers Digest; September 1973; pages 150–154.

1935 Owens establishes four world's track records in one afternoon

When Jesse Owens graduated from East Technical High School of Cleveland, Ohio, he had established three national high school records in track. At Ohio State University, Jesse ran like the wind and broke a few more world marks. And in the 1936 Olympic games at Berlin the lithe Negro speedster — who had by now acquired the nickname of *The Ebony Express* — built imperishable fame by winning four gold medals!

Nevertheless, the sum total of all this glorious achievement pales beside the performance of Jesse Owens on May 25, 1935, at the Big Ten conference championships held at Ann Arbor, Michigan.

Getting up from a sickbed, Jesse in his first event ran the 100-yard dash in 9.4 seconds, to tie the world's record.

Ten minutes later in the broad jump, Jesse leaped 26 feet eight and one quarter inches *on his first try* to best the world's record.

Nine minutes later, running in the 220-yard dash, Jesse sped down the course in 20.3 seconds to smash another world's record.

And just about 45 minutes after he had participated in the first event, Jesse negotiated the 220-yard hurdles in 22.6 seconds, shattering still another world's record.

In one single afternoon — within the space of three quarters of an hour — Jesse Owens established world records in four events. In this century, no other trackman has ever set more than one world's record in any one day.

Source: Ann Arbor (Michigan) News; May 25, 1960; page 36, column 1.

1935 Barna wins his fifteenth world title in table tennis

Never in the 80-year history of the paddle game has one man dominated the field as did Viktor Barna in the late 1920's and mid-30's. He won 15 championship crowns—and if Europe hadn't been in turmoil, he might have won even more.

Between 1930 and 1935, Barna won the world singles title five times — a record that still stands. Using different partners in several tournaments, he copped the world's doubles title eight times — another record performance. And for good measure, he twice joined a female partner to win the mixed doubles.

When Viktor was at his peak, his backhand flick just swept opponents off the courts. He is reputed to have had the best backhand of any player that ever lived. His smashing drives propelled the ball at a speed of 50 miles per hour.

Source: "The Official Encyclopedia of Sports"; John Lowell Pratt and Jim Benagh; Franklin Watts, Inc.; 1964; page 277.

1935 Ruth hits three home runs in one game — numbers 712, 713, and 714 of his career

Well before the 1935 season began, Babe Ruth's golden career had begun to tarnish. Plagued by age and personal problems, the legendary Yankee slugger had become little more than a curiosity piece when he was traded to the Boston Braves. By mid-May of that year, the man who in 1927 had hit 60 homers was batting a dismal .179, and he was spending most of his time on the bench.

On May 25, 1935, the 40-year-old Bambino took the field against the Pirates in Pittsburgh. On his first trip to the plate, he cracked a long homer into the right-field stands. A few innings later, his bat sent another fastball soaring into the bleachers. Next time up, Ruth banged out a single that scored a run.

When the Babe stepped to the plate again late in the game, the fans were clamoring for another four-bagger. The old Sultan of Swat dug in, then brought the crowd to its feet with a towering blast to right that went clear out of Forbes Field. No one had ever hit a ball over those right-field stands before.

As Ruth rounded the bases, few could guess that this homer, number 714, would be his last. But the three home runs he hit that day were a fitting finale to a career performance without equal in baseball. He was a great pitcher in his youth. His .342 lifetime batting average and 714 home runs made him baseball's all-time great at the bat, and now Ruth left the game in a final blaze of glory.

Source: "Babe Ruth"; Martin Weldon; Crowell; 1948.

1936 Mary Joyce travels 1,000 miles by dog sled

The rigors of the frozen North are famed in song and story. A dog-sled trip of even 100 miles holds its terrors for even a strong man enured to the biting cold and fierce winds of the frigid zone.

Yet on Thursday, March 26, 1936, in the dead of the Arctic winter, one 27-year-old Alaskan girl drove her dog sled into Fairbanks, Alaska, from distant Taku — a trip of 1,000 miles. She had left her hunting lodge which was 40 miles from Juneau on December 22, 1935, heading into the treacherous mountains, the blizzards, and the loneliness which lay ahead. For about three months, without any human aid, she battled the elements, rarely encountering weather any milder than 34 degrees below zero, and hitting days when the thermometer dropped to 60 below.

Neatly attired in dark blue hiking trousers, heavy blue woolen jacket, snug-fitting black fur cap and knee-length moccasins, Miss Joyce presented a striking picture as she swung down the home stretch of the Richardson Highway into Fairbanks, where standing exultantly in front of her team of five huskies, she was acclaimed by the town's notables.

Source: Fairbanks Daily News-Miner; March 26, 1936; page 1.

1936 Blake surf rides a wave for almost a mile

In popular fancy, good surfers are imagined capable of riding a wave for several miles. This is a misconception, for even at Honolulu's Waikiki Beach, generally considered to offer the finest surfing conditions in the world, the average ride is no more than 200 yards. Occasionally, though, when surf and tide conditions are right, longer rides become possible—at least for the best surfers, *if* they are lucky enough to be in the right place at the right time.

Commonplace 200-yard rides take place at Waikiki when the surf is running at "blow-hole-break," which is just about every day. (A break is a point where a wave slows, builds up, and then scatters.) At "first-break," which occurs somewhat less often, a good surfer can make 300 yards. When the surf breaks at Kalahuewehe, or "castle-break," he can make 500 yards, but this condition occurs only about three times a year. Even less frequent is "chuna-break," a condition when half-mile rides are possible. The longest rides of all occur when the surf comes in at "zero-break," something that very rarely happens.

It did happen, though, just before sundown one evening early in June 1936, and Tom Blake, probably the top surfer of all time, was on the spot and ready. In fact, Tom had been ready and waiting for a chance like this for six years.

The tide was running extremely high off Waikiki that day, so Blake knew something big was coming; though, of course, he had no way of predicting that it would be "zero-break." Along with several other skilled surfers, he took to the water

and calmly edged his board into position far out at the mouth of Waikiki Bay.

Watching intently, Blake suddenly observed a set of monster waves rearing up about a half-mile off. Here, indeed, was the big one!

Catching the second wave of the set, Blake began riding in toward the beach atop a 25-foot-high solid wall of water stretching across the full width of Waikiki Bay. None of his companions made it, but Blake, progressing rapidly from "first-break-south-castle" through "public-baths break" and "chuna-break," soon reached the shore opposite Lalani Village. He had completed a surf ride of about a mile, the longest ever recorded.

Source: Paradise of the Pacific; volume 48 (October 1936); page 27.

1937 Raglan sets 27,778 bricks in eight hours

Paving bricks were once widely used as a road-surfacing material. Slightly larger than ordinary construction bricks, they measured about 2-1/2 by 4 by 9 inches, and each weighed about 9 pounds. When a road or street was being surfaced, a man called a brick-dropper carefully set each paving brick into place by hand. When assisted by helpers who kept him supplied with fresh bricks, a good brick-dropper could set, on the average, about 15,000 bricks a day.

During the 1930s, many American city streets were still paved with brick. At that time, because of the Depression, a considerable number of road-building and street-surfacing projects were carried out by the Works Progress Administration. Since the W.P.A. was run by the Federal government and was frankly dedicated to keeping unemployed people busy, W.P.A. jobs soon developed a bad reputation in some circles. For many people, the letters W.P.A. became a synonym for make-work, incompetence, and government-subsidized laziness.

Thus it is ironic to learn that the fastest brick-dropper in history was a W.P.A. man by the name of Joe Raglan. He was employed at the grand salary of $52 a month on the Piggot Avenue street-paving project in East St. Louis, Illinois.

Everyone on the job knew Joe Raglan was fast. One day in March 1937, he set out to demonstrate just how fast he really was. With helpers handing him four bricks at a time, he worked steadily through the day, stopping only for lunch. His skilled hands seemed to be flying. At the end of eight hours, Raglan's co-workers tallied up the results: Joe had set 27,778 bricks into place—about 12,000 more than what was considered a superior day's work.

Source: St. Louis Post-Dispatch; March 14, 1937.

1937 Morris skips rope 22,806 times in two hours

Thomas Morris had a strange mode of locomotion.
He got a great kick out of skipping rope, and once he traveled from Melbourne to Adelaide and back, a distance of 1,000 miles, skipping rope all the way.

On November 21, 1937, Morris began skipping before a timer in Sydney, Australia. Morris wanted to make some sort of an official test as to his prowess and speed. He set off at a rate of 200 beats a minute, better than three skips every single second. The pace was so grueling that his audience was stunned into silence. After one hour had passed, it was recorded that Morris had completed 12,000 skips. Since he was still fresh, he decided to go on for another hour, and without missing a beat, he continued. At the finish, his timers were as worn out as he was. For they had tallied an astonishing 22,806 skips. If each skip were accounted as the step of an average man, Thomas Morris, in those two hours, would have walked about 12 miles!

Source: Reuters dispatch; November 21, 1937.

1937 Sohn glides to earth on canvas wings from almost four miles up

Man has always been intrigued by the thought of flying through his own physical power, without the aid of any heavy mechanism. The man who has come closest to that dream was Clem Sohn.

Sohn, an air-show performer in the 1930's, had perfected a way of gliding through the air with home-made wings. He had himself dropped from an airplane at a height of approximately 20,000 feet, and then he would float downward some three miles or so until he was but 800 or 1,000 feet from the ground, at which point he would open up his parachute for the final descent.

Clem, who hailed from Lansing, Michigan, made his

wings out of zephyr cloth and mounted them on steel tubes to form a large web which was clasped to his hips. A loose cloth formed another web between his legs. His large goggles gave him an appearance which justifiably led to his becoming known as *"The Batman."*

Sohn's amazing act came to an end on April 25, 1937, in Vincennes, France. Before taking off, Clem had remarked, "I feel as safe as you would in your grandmother's kitchen." But during his descent on that day, his parachute didn't open. A terror-stricken crowd of 100,000 watched him frantically tug on the ripcord of his emergency chute, but that failed, too; and Clem Sohn, only 26 years old, plunged to his death.

Source: *New York Times; April 26, 1937; page 1, column 4.*

1937 Day bowls 33 consecutive strikes

In bowling, knocking down all the pins with one ball is called a *strike*. To bowl a perfect game, player must throw 12 strikes in a row. Such a perfect performance has been accomplished now and then, but the bowling of a perfect game is a rarity. It is estimated that perfect games occur just about once in every 450,000 tries.

During an exhibition at Price Hall in Cincinnati, Ohio, in 1937, Ned Day of West Allis, Wisconsin, bowled 33 strikes in a row! This was equivalent to bowling almost three perfect games in succession.

Source: Colliers Magazine; June 3, 1944; page 21.

1937 Varipapa bowls two balls at one time

After he came to the United States in 1903 from his native Carfizzi, Italy, Andy Varipapa started bowling. He was still going strong in the 1960's. During that long span there was hardly any bowling title worth winning that Andy didn't carry off at one time or another. During his career, he rolled more than 70 perfect games, and, of course, was chosen for bowling's Hall of Fame.

But Andy, who resided in Hempstead, New York, liked a break from serious, big-time bowling; and for fun, he would put on exhibitions to display his incomparable array of trick shots. His favorite stunt was to bowl two balls at one time, one from each hand. One ball would pick off the No. 7 pin at deep left, and the other would pick off the No. 10 pin in deep right.

In his favorite version of this trick—for Andy had more than one way of knocking off the 7-10 split—he let go with one ball from his left hand moments before releasing the other ball from his right hand. Since Andy was right-handed, the ball that left his right hand moved a bit faster than the other, and hooked to the left. The two balls then crossed well down the alley and headed for opposite gutters. But Varipapa had so much spin on each of the spheres that they curved back and *crossed each other a second time.* Thus the ball from the left hand hit the No. 7 pin on the left side, while the ball from the right hand picked up the No. 10 pin.

That shot, with its zigzag trip down the alley, fooled

everybody— even the best bowlers. Andy jokingly called it "The Double Cross."

Source: New York World-Telegram weekend magazine, Metropolitan; March 6, 1937; page 12.

1938 Armstrong holds three world's boxing championships at the same time

If a boxer happens to be the best in his class, he will probably get to the top of the heap—in his class. However, Henry Armstrong of St. Louis, Missouri, hopped to the top of three boxing heaps all within less than a year.

On October 29, 1937, Henry Armstrong became the world's featherweight champion by knocking out Petey Sarron in the sixth round of a fight for the title.

Seven months later, on May 31, 1938, Armstrong took the world's welterweight crown away from Barney Ross in a 15-round decision.

Two and one-half months later, on August 17, 1938, Armstrong, having now pared himself down to 134 pounds, met the rugged Lou Ambers at Madison Square Garden to fight for the lightweight championship of the world, and won the title on a decision.

No one else has ever simultaneously held three world's championships in boxing!

Henry Armstrong had been brought up in the slums of St. Louis as just another poor, undernourished kid named Henry Jackson. After a playground scuffle, the little first-grader came home with a bloodied face. His mother slapped him hard, and said, "If you have to fight, then learn *how* to fight."

Henry Armstrong certainly did.

Source: Sport Magazine; June, 1963; pages 28-29.

1938 Hall scores three goals in three and one half minutes of soccer

Soccer is a low-scoring game—especially in international matches. Generally, a score will run two goals or three goals a game, rarely as many as six. So the nonpareil outburst by a British stalwart, G. W. Hall, must rank among the greatest soccer feats of all time.

On November 16, 1938, England stunned its arch-rival Ireland in a one-sided contest that ended 7-0. What was remarkable was that three of those goals were scored by one player in the space of three and a half minutes. Never in major competition has any soccer player tallied in such a rat-a-tat fashion.

With England leading 1-0 in the first half, 40,000 witnesses

at the Old Trafford stadium in Manchester saw London's inside-right turn the trick. Hall scored his initial tally set up in front of the goal-mouth by his brilliant team-mate, Stanley Matthews. Moments after the ensuing kick-off, Hall scored again — this time on a low corner shot from inside left. When the ball was put back in play, the Irish goalie was determined to stop the barrage. Charged with more enthusiasm than wisdom, he ventured out too far after Hall, and the net was an easy target. Hall tallied again, and the crowd went wild!

But Hall wasn't through. Ten minutes after the intermission, the Britisher connected again with a fine spinning shot that he hooked in with his back turned to the goalie.

And Willie scored still once more when the redoubtable Matthews, dribbling past two men, flicked a pass which Hall converted. That made five for Willie for the afternoon.

Source: Encyclopedia of Association Football; Maurice Golesworthy;
Robert Hale, Ltd.; 1967; page 96.
The Times of London; November 17, 1938; page 6, column 1.

1938 Cote covers ten miles on snowshoes in a little over an hour

Gerard Cote was an athlete for all seasons. In warm weather, he was a distance runner who had won the famous 26-mile Boston Marathon three times. In winter, he was a snowshoer.

One fine day in 1938, the French Canadian ventured down to Montreal from his home in St. Hyacinthe for the national championships. Wearing standard 10" by 33" snowshoes, the 24-year-old newsboy, who stood only five feet, six inches tall and weighed a mere 130 pounds, clomped over the 10-mile course in 63 minutes and 45 seconds — a record performance.

Source: Letter from Raoul Charbonneau, Secretary, Canadian Snowshoer's Union; February 19, 1969.

1938 Vander Meer hurls two consecutive no-hitters

On the night of June 15, 1938, nearly 40,000 fans crowded Brooklyn's Ebbets Field. The attraction was twofold: this was the first Dodger home game to be played under the lights; and the opposing hurler, Cincinnati's Johnny Vander Meer, had thrown a no-hitter against the Boston Bees in his last start.

Few of the fans gave much thought to whether the Reds' ace could duplicate his feat of four days before. No one had ever pitched two consecutive no-hitters. On the contrary, many a hurler had followed his masterpiece with a dreadful performance.

But Vander Meer mowed down the Dodgers inning after inning. As Johnny came out to the mound for the bottom of the ninth, the tension in the ball park was at fever pitch. Only three outs stood between him and baseball immortality.

Trying to rear back for a little extra zip on his fastball, the weakening pitcher suddenly lost the plate. Though he managed to retire two men, he also walked three. The sixth batter to face him that inning was Leo Durocher, the Dodger shortstop. Vander Meer had one great pitch left in his weary left arm, and Durocher popped it weakly into short center field. Harry Craft raced in and made the catch, and Vander Meer had his second no-hitter in a row. No one had ever done it before, and no one has done it since.

Source: New York Times; June 16, 1938.

1938 Cunningham, a cripple, becomes the world's best miler

When he was eight years old, Glenn Cunningham was trapped in a fire which left him horribly burned. The worst

charred parts of his body were his legs. All the toes of
his left foot were lost, as well as much of the muscle tissue.
Doctors told the young lad that he might never walk again.

But young Cunningham had remarkable fortitude, and he
set himself to the arduous task of relearning to walk.
After he had gained locomotion, Glenn was not content with
just walking: he learned how to run, too. Then he learned
how to run fast.

Before he graduated from high school in Elkhart, Kansas,
he could run a mile in four minutes and 24.7 seconds. He
was the fastest schoolboy in the United States.

Later, in 1934, at the University of Kansas, Cunningham
set a world's record in the mile run (4:06.8), and two years
later, Glenn set another record in the half mile (1:49.7). His
indoor mile of 4:04.4, made in 1938, stood as a record for
many years.

The boy who could not walk wound up teaching his
contemporaries something about running. He developed
his own method of pacing, building himself up for his
sprinting finish. He would run the last quarter of the mile
in the unheard of clocking of under one minute. It was
Glenn's style, adopted and modified by the sprinters who
succeeded him, that opened the way for the under-four-
minute runs that once seemed beyond human capability.

Source. "Modern Track & Field"; J. Kenneth Doherty; Prentice-Hall, Inc.; 1955;
pages 188-199.

1940 Abbye Stockton lifts a man over her head on her hands

At five feet, one inch and weighing no more than 118 pounds, Abbye Stockton looked petite and frail next to the strongmen with whom she performed. But the little lady from Santa Monica, California, was all muscle.

For example, in the three standard weight-lifting events, Miss Stockton could press 110 pounds, snatch 100 pounds, and clean-and-jerk 140.

In the late 1940's, she toured the country with her husband, Les, a 185-pounder. As she stood upright, he would stand on her shoulders. He would then flip into a handstand using Abbye's palms for a base, and Abbye would hold him up—with one hand—for as much as 30 seconds. This in itself was not a new feat; circus performers had been doing it for years. But the stunt had always been performed by an Amazonian female heavyweight, who supported a very light man. Abbye Stockton weighed 67 pounds less than the man she was holding up!

Source: Letter from John Grimek, Strength and Health Magazine; June 10, 1968. Letter from Abbye Stockton; July 7, 1968.

1940 Sigmund swims continuously for 89 hours and 48 minutes

At 7:22 p.m., July 25, 1940, John Sigmund lowered himself into the Mississippi River at St. Louis, Missouri, and set out on one of the most adventuresome swims ever attempted. The 30-year-old St. Louis butcher would swim for 89 hours and 48 minutes before being pulled out of the water on July 28, dazed and exhausted, at Caruthersville, Missouri.

The Mississippi River is so muddy that floating objects often can't be seen. During his stint, Sigmund injured a leg on a submerged log. Some time later, the waves of a passing barge washed him against his accompanying cabin cruiser and nearly knocked him unconscious. And to add to his travail, on the very last night of his journey, Sigmund wandered three miles off course when he mistakenly entered one of the Mississippi's tributaries.

For energy, his wife, Catherine, frequently furnished him with candy bars. It was only through her constant prodding during the final 25 miles that the exhausted Sigmund was prevented from falling asleep in the water. At the finish—292 miles from his starting point, an all-time distance record—hundreds of bystanders cheered. But Sigmund could not acknowledge their acclaim. Unable to either walk or talk, he was carried off by friends.

Nevertheless, the next day John showed no ill effects. The damage—a sun-blistered face, wobbly legs, and aching muscles—would quickly pass away.

Source: St. Louis Post-Dispatch; July 29, 1940; page 3-A, column 2.

1940 Bauman husks 46.71 bushels of corn in 80 minutes

In rural America, farmers were wont to turn anything into a sport. There were contests in roping calves; there were contests in chasing and catching greased pigs; and there were contests in shearing sheep. Thus it could be expected

that in the midwestern corn belt—before the machine age took over — the husking bee became a popular competition.

The champion husker of all time was one Irving Bauman of Woodford County, Illinois, who earned his title in 1940 on a farm near Davenport, Iowa. Matched against the best huskers of Nebraska and Iowa, Irving began mowing the cornfield on Henry Keppy's farm as if he were a human scythe. An average paid farmhand would husk just about four bushels an hour. On October 30, the 27-year-old Bauman clipped that many off the stalks in just about five minutes.

Before his 80 minutes were up, the sweaty Bauman, though ready to keel over, had broken all records. He had garnered a haul of 46.71 bushels.

Source: Davenport (Iowa) Democrat & Leader; October 31, 1940; page 24, col. 3.

1941 DiMaggio hits safely in 56 straight baseball games

On May 15, 1941, Joe DiMaggio, playing for the New York Yankees, got up to bat and slapped a single against the Chicago White Sox pitcher, Edgar Smith. It was an unremarkable hit and nobody paid much attention to it. But that sock was the beginning of the longest hitting streak ever made in baseball.

For the next few weeks, Joltin' Joe kept popping hits day after day and game after game. Before his bat went silent, three months had passed. Joe had hit safely in 56 consecutive games. The previous record had been held by Willie Keeler who, playing for the old Baltimore Orioles, had hit safely in 44 consecutive games.

After he topped Keeler's record, Joe got better and better. Now he was hitting two, three, and even four hits a game instead of just the one hit he needed to maintain the pace. On July 16, DiMaggio blasted the Cleveland pitcher for three hits in three times at bat. His teammates, too, were riding the crest of his streak, winning 30 out of their last 35 games.

During his phenomenal run, DiMaggio had gone to bat 223 times. He had hit safely 91 times, an average of .408. The Yankee Clipper had slammed out 16 doubles, four triples, and 15 home runs!

Can DiMaggio's record ever be bettered? Probably not. Modern-day players rarely hit over .340, and are involved in many night games. It is conceded that night ball is much harder on batters. During his streak, DiMaggio played only four times under the arc lights. Nevertheless, in any day or age, Joe's feat must be considered a record of proportions.

Source: "Little Red Book of Baseball"; 1967 edition; Elias Sports Bureau, Inc.; page 155.

1943 Victoria Zacchini travels 200 feet as a human cannonball

Few circus events require the daring and poise of the stunt which has come to be known as "The Human Cannonball." This act employs lots of phony noise and smoke, and then jets a human being into space from the mouth of a cannon.

Despite the hoopla, the successful completion of this act depends on exact coordination between the person who is being shot, the huge spring that catapults him, and the assistants in charge of the mechanism. The "cannonball" must maintain his poise while traveling through the air— and he travels faster than a speeding automobile. He is supposed to land in a net some distance away, but if the propulsion is weak or there is some other flaw, he can fall short of that distance with disastrous results. Over 30 human "bullets" have died during the 20th century.

During April of 1943, in New York's Polo Grounds, Victoria Zacchini was shot from the barrel of the 22-foot silver cannon at a speed of well over 100 miles an hour. The 110-pound human projectile climbed to a height of over 100 feet and then fell safely into a net 200 feet away — a record shot!

Source: Associated Press dispatch; April 28, 1943.

1943 Poon Lim survives for 133 days on a life raft

On November 23, 1942, the S. S. Lomond, an English merchant manned by a crew of 55, was torpedoed in the South Atlantic. Only one of the seamen survived—a 25-year-old Chinese by the name of Poon Lim. He had been catapulted off the deck by an explosion of such force that the very clothes were blown from his back.

Lim swam in the neighborhood of the wreck for two hours, and then grabbed a drifting life raft on which he survived for 133 days, naked and exposed to the elements. The raft carried enough food and water for him to live through 60 days. After that, his very life depended on the fish he could catch.

Poon fashioned a hook from a spring which he extracted from the raft's flashlight, and he trolled for small fish. He used these small ones as bait for larger game. Occasionally, he would grab at and catch a sea gull for a meatier meal.

But hunger was not his only trial. Verily, Poon Lim was like Coleridge's "ancient mariner," who bemoaned:

> Alone, alone, oh! all alone,
>   Alone on a wide, wide sea;
> And never a saint took pity on
>   My soul in agony.

For more than four months, Lim drifted through calm and squall, and at long last neared the coast of Brazil. On April 5, 1943, he was spotted by some fishermen who took him aboard. He was palpably ill, and his legs were wobbly, but yet his rescuers found it hard to believe that this 5-foot,

5-inch little mite of a man could have possibly endured through better than a third of a year on an exposed raft, bobbing at random in the middle of the ocean.

When the story reached Britain the tale met with a different reception. The British knew about the torpedoing of the S.S. Lomond. King George VI, deeply impressed with Poon's fortitude, presented him in 1943 with England's highest civilian award, the British Empire medal. Speaking of his incredible record, Poon Lim said "I hope no one will ever have to break it."

Source: New York Times; July 17, 1943; page 6, column 4.

1946 Calverley's 55-foot basketball shot ties tournament game

In basketball, it's size that counts. That's why oddsmakers made the five giants from Bowling Green a 12-point favorite over little Rhode Island State on March 14, 1946, in the opening game of the National Invitation Tournament in New York City. A record 18,548 fans crowded the old 49th Street Madison Square Garden. Standing five-foot-ten, Ernie Calverley of underdog Rhode Island jumped

against the six-foot-eleven Don Otten of the Ohioans
at the tipoff.

Rhode Island State surprised, and the game was close
all the way. On 13 occasions, the score was tied. Then, with

3:20 minutes left on the clock, the Ohioans lost Otten on fouls. But Bowling Green still had the height to control the game. With only ten seconds remaining, Bowling Green held onto a 74-72 lead. As the tension mounted, Rhode Island moved the ball down the court. In order to stop the advance, a Bowling Green player barged in and risked a one-shot foul—a pretty smart maneuver, for under the rules in effect at the time, if Rhode Island chose to shoot the foul, they would lose the game even if their player had sank his foul shot. Time would just run out.

So Rhode Island elected to waive the foul shot, and took possession of the ball. Only three seconds were left now to move the ball the full length of the court, and make a basket. It was a practical impossibility. The Bowling Green players tightened their web around the Rhode Islanders. Somehow, Calverley broke loose. He was well behind the mid-court line when a teammate threw the ball to him. Almost without a pause, Calverley let fly for the basket—a target which seemed miles away. Here was a desperation shot if there ever was one. But Ernie's long-distance two-hander executed a perfect parabola and descended cleanly through the mesh, not even touching the rim. Calverley had tied the game, and the Garden broke loose in pandemonium!

After that, in the overtime, Bowling Green, still in the throes of shock, was no match for the little Rams, who won by a final score of 82 to 79.

Opinions differ as to the exact point from which Calverley let fly. The ball zoomed at least 50 feet—no one disputes that. However, some observers estimated the distance at 65 feet. A Garden official close to the scene claimed that he recalled the exact point from which the ball took off, and the officials measured it at 55 feet. But wherever it was, Ernie had certainly made the most famous basketball shot in history.

Source: "Madison Square Garden Hall of Fame Book;" edited by Joe Val; Robert W. Kelly Publishing Corp.; 1967; page 86.

1946 Sullivan kicks 100 goals in rugby for eighteenth consecutive season

James Sullivan of Cardiff, Wales, began his professional
career as a rugby player in 1921 when he was just seventeen.
That season, he scored 108 goals and 222 points, and he
instantly became a star on the Wigan team in the Rugby
League of Northern England.

Thereafter, for the next 17 years, Sullivan kicked
over 100 goals a year. His total point score averaged
300 per annum.

In 1933, the redoubtable Sullivan scored an even
200 goals. By 1946, the Welsh fullback, then 42 years
old, had established all-time records in major league rugby
with 2,955 goals and 6,192 points.

Source: Encyclopedia Britannica; Encyclopedia Britannica, Inc.; 1966;
Volume 9, page 593.

1947 Wistert becomes third brother in family to win All-American football honors

It certainly ran in the family. Evidently, they were all cast from the same mold for each of them played tackle, and all three Wisterts attended the same school—the University of Michigan.

In 1933, Francis was voted All-American and started a trend. He played football so well that years later historians selected him for a place in the National Football Foundation's Hall of Fame.

In 1942, along came Albert; he, too, made a mark for himself and was voted All-American honors.

The youngest, Alvin, followed in his brothers' footsteps, but followed rather late. In 1947, *at age 32*, he achieved All-American honors. Alvin repeated in 1948.

All in all, the three Wisterts competed in 80 contests. The teams they were on scored 68 victories, and were defeated only eight times. Four of the games ended in ties.

Source: "The Big Ten"; Kenneth L. (Tug) Wilson and Jerry Bronfield; Prentice-Hall Inc.; 1967; page 81.

1947 Lewis wins his 6,200th wrestling match

In 1904, a fourteen-year-old youngster by the name of Robert Friedrich entered the professional wrestling ring and won his first match. In order to withhold his activity from his parents, he was billed under the name of Ed Lewis. During a career lasting 43 years, Strangler Lewis, as he came to be known, won more than 6,200 matches. During this long period, Lewis was defeated only 33 times.

It would be hardly disputable to claim that Ed Lewis was the greatest professional wrestler who ever lived. He ruled the roost in an era when professional wrestling was a legitimate sport. There would be little point in comparing his record with the comics who cavort around the ring today; for professional wrestlers in this age of television merely present well-rehearsed performances which are dramatized to please the viewing crowd. Professional wrestling today is a far cry from 1916, when on July 4, Lewis battled for five and one-half hours in an Omaha arena against champion Joe Stecker. That match may not have been spectacular, but it was real, and it was grueling. Nor could the match have been very satisfying to either the audience or to the contestants, because the bout wound up in a draw.

In 1920, the Strangler—who, by the way, got his moniker because of his deadly headlock—met Stecker again at the 71st Regiment Armory in New York. This time he won the coveted championship. Lewis continued as top man throughout the 1920's, the glamour era of American sports, which was blazoned with names like Babe Ruth, Bill Tilden, Red Grange, Bobby Jones and Jack Dempsey. In that era, Lewis enjoyed similar popularity.

Once, Lewis offered to meet Dempsey in a ring; Dempsey could do the boxing, and Lewis would do the wrestling. Jack Dempsey turned down the challenge. No wonder! The Strangler, who weighed around 260 pounds, had a neck that measured 21 inches, and a grip that was like a steel vise.

To get an idea of the Strangler's drawing power with the public, he demanded and received $125,000 guarantees on certain occasions.

The boy from Madison, Wisconsin, certainly made good. During his career as a wrestler, Ed Lewis earned over $4,000,000.

Source: New York Times; August 8, 1966; page 27, column 1.

1948 Mathias wins the Olympic decathlon at age 17

No title is held in greater esteem than the Olympic decathlon. The champion in this event is generally regarded as the greatest athlete in the world. There is no doubt that the performances in the 1968 decathlon in Mexico City were watched on television by more viewers than any other Olympic event. The decathlon performer must be able to run, to jump, and to throw. He must be able to sprint, and to have sufficient endurance to last a long distance. He must blend agility with strength.

Just a few months before he was tapped to carry the hopes of the United States in the 1948 Olympics in London, 17-year-old Bob Mathias had never touched a javelin. Nor had he ever pole-vaulted. And to top off his inexperience, the 400-meter distance and the 1,500-meter distance were quite unfamiliar. His enthusiastic high school coach suggested to his young charge that he try out for the Olympic team anyhow. The lad weighed 190 pounds, was strong, willing, and was an exceptionally good competitor. Bob Mathias was the cool type. The coach believed that he wouldn't make the team, but that he would gain valuable experience for the next competition, four years later.

However, Mathias exceeded everyone's hopes, including his own. He won the very first decathlon meet he entered, defeating several well-known college stars. Less than a month later, he won the U.S. championship. In a short six weeks, the boy found himself in the international arena in London.

Here Mathias took on the world's best as if he were a veteran. The schoolboy ran the 100 meters in 11.2 seconds; the 400 meters in 51.7 seconds; the rugged 1,500 meters in 5 minutes and 11 seconds; the 110-meter hurdles in 15.7 seconds. He broad-jumped 21 feet 8 inches; high-jumped 6 feet 1¼ inches, and pole-vaulted 11 feet 5½ inches. In the weight events, he threw the javelin 165 feet 1 inch; the shot put, 42 feet 9 inches; and he hurled the discus 144 feet 4 inches. His 7,139 points easily led the field.

When the two-day ordeal ended on August 6, an onlooker

asked Bob what he would do to celebrate his victory. "Start shaving, I guess," said Bob.

Source: "Story of the Olympic Games"; John Kieran and Arthur Daley; Lippincott; 1965; pages 207-209.

1948 Fanny Blankers-Koen wins four Olympic gold medals

When Fanny Blankers-Koen stepped up to the starting line at Wembley Stadium in London during the 1948 Olympics, few in the stands would guess that this attractive blonde was a housewife and the mother of two young children. When the gun blasted off, the trim Hollander dashed to the forefront, and stayed there until she reached the tape—the winner in the 100-meter dash in 11.9 seconds.

Mrs. Blankers-Koen then proceeded to carry off the honors in the 200-meter dash, covering the distance in 24.4 seconds.

In negotiating the 80-meter hurdles, she established an Olympic record of 11.2 seconds.

And to top off her performance, Fanny led the 400-meter relay team from the Netherlands to a first-place victory. The Dutch housewife had carted off four gold medals within a week's time—an Olympic record.

But there is more to be said. Unfortunately, the Olympic rules limited the blonde streak to entering three individual events. At a time when Fanny Blankers-Koen held the world's record in both the broad jump and the high jump, had she been allowed to compete in these events, it is safe to say that she would have done fairly well.

Source: "An Illustrated History of the Olympics"; Richard Schaap; Alfred Knopf; 1963; pages 240-241.

1950 Capilla executes four and a half somersaults in a 33-foot platform dive

On a fine day in 1950, in the Chapultepec Club in
Mexico City, Joaquin Capilla executed a four and one-half
somersault dive off the 10-meter-high diving board.
Within the space of just about 33 feet, the little acrobat
twirled himself around head-first four times, and then
another half-time before completing his plunge.

This dive is so difficult that it isn't even listed in the
international scoring system. No wonder! No other man
before or since has executed this dive.

Source: Letter from Mexican Olympic Committee; November 18, 1968.

1950 Ross paddles across the English Channel in four hours and seven minutes

The kayak was invented by the Eskimos for hunting trips in the stilled icy seas of the Far North. Certainly this rather frail craft was not conceived to battle the churning swells and tidal currents of the English Channel. But civilized man, in order to evidence his mastery of nature, has always sought new ways to pit brain and muscle against seemingly unconquerable forces. And so the men of our day have taken to cross the Channel in kayaks. The fact is it's been done several times.

In this exercise, none was faster than one Henry Ross, an engineer from Surrey, England. Setting out from Gris Nez in France on a bright morning, August 10, 1950, Ross began to paddle toward Dover. It was the same 22-mile route taken by most Channel swimmers.

Aided by ideal weather and driven by furious determination, the 37-year-old Ross moved much faster than even he had planned. When he pulled into Dover only four hours and seven minutes after leaving France, he learned that he had bested the then existing record by a full 50 minutes.

Source: London Daily Herald; August 11, 1950; page 1, column 6.

1950 Mildred Didrikson Zaharias proves a champion in track, golf, and baseball

In 1950, the Associated Press polled its sports writers and sportscasters to choose the greatest female athlete of the first half of the 20th century. The Associated Press people selected "Babe" Didrikson Zaharias (née Mildred Didrikson). It was an easy choice, for the Babe from Beaumont, Texas, was generally considered to be the greatest woman athlete who ever lived. She could handle a javelin, a golf club, a tennis racquet, a basketball, a bowling ball, or a baseball with equal ease and proficiency.

The Babe first came into national prominence as a basketball player. During her teens, she was nominated on All-America teams for three straight years, though she stood merely a shade over five feet tall. In one of her games, she scored over 100 points.

In 1932, Mildred entered the Amateur Athletic Union national track championships as a one-woman track team representing the Employers Casualty Company of Dallas. Other competing teams consisted of 10 to 22 members. Yet on that weekend in Chicago, the 18-year-old Babe entered eight events and scored points in seven. She won five outright, setting three world records in the process. Before the close of 1932, the 105-pound girl added two Olympic titles to her collection of medals, winning the javelin throw and the hurdles.

In baseball, Mildred toured the country with a professional barnstorming team—a team composed only of men; and she played only against men. But the Babe could throw a ball

almost 300 feet on a straight line.

She mastered tennis, too, but was outlawed from competition because she was deemed a professional.

In bowling, she generally averaged a hefty 170; but it was once recorded that she rolled a 237.

As the Babe grew older, she found her favorite sport in golf. During her career, she won more than 50 major tournaments. She once ran up a streak of 17 tournament victories. With the help of a tail wind, she once drove a ball 346 yards!

In 1954, after undergoing an operation for cancer, Mildred Zaharias won her third National Open. Had her brilliant career not been cut short by the dread killer, Mrs. Zaharias, who passed away in 1956 at the age of 43, would have undoubtedly added still more laurels.

Source: "This Life I've Led"; Babe Didrikson Zaharias with Harry Paxton; A. S. Barnes & Co., Inc.; 1955.

1951 Walcott wins the heavyweight boxing title at age 37

A boxer is generally in his prime during his mid-twenties. By the time he has hit twenty-nine he is, as a rule, considered a has-been, ready for retirement.

But not Jersey Joe Walcott. On July 18, 1951, when he entered the ring against the faster, more agile Ezzard Charles, Jersey Joe was challenging the champ for the third time. Twice before, Walcott had tried and lost. Moreover, Walcott had twice lost to former champ Joe Louis. After a total of four failures—in itself a record for trying to take the heavyweight title—Walcott had resigned from the ring.

That Jersey Joe would venture a championship fight for the fifth time was astonishing; and the odds of six to one against him reflected how fistic experts regarded his chances.

Ezzard Charles had seemed a cinch to win. He had come to fight with a string of 24 straight wins behind him. Walcott, the "has-been" and father of six, had gone into the ring with a lot of bills to pay. He had come out of retirement because he needed the money.

The bout was held in Pittsburgh's Forbes Field. A goodly crowd of 28,000 attended and a television audience of 60 million watched. Walcott, 194 pounds, got off to a slow start. But in the third round he opened up a cut under Charles' eye. In the next three rounds, Joe racked up points, and in the seventh, the "old man" lured the champ into a trap. Feinting a body punch, Joe let go with a short, crisp hook—only about six inches—to Charles' jaw. Ezzard fell, tried to rise, then toppled again. The fight was over.

Thus Jersey Joe, a veteran of 21 years in the ring and thirty-seven years old, became the oldest man ever to win the world's heavyweight title.

Source: The New York Times; July 19, 1951; page 27, column 1.
"Ring Record Book"; Nat Fleischer; Ring Book Shop; 1967; page 60.

1952 Mosienko scores three goals in 21 seconds in a professional hockey game

In a lackluster professional hockey game in New York on March 23, 1952, the New York Rangers were pitted against the Chicago Black Hawks. The visitors were

behind, 6 to 2, in the final period; some of the more than 3,000 fans who had come to see the game had already left the dreary spectacle. The Rangers had the game virtually won. What was there to stay for?

Then, with less than 14 minutes to play, right wing Bill Mosienko, thirty years old, picked up a pass from teammate Gus Bodnar and rapped in a goal.

On the ensuing face-off, Bodnar again got the puck to Mosienko, and the pint-sized 160-pounder smashed in goal No. 2. Only 11 seconds had separated the two tallies. The score now stood at 6 to 4.

On the next face-off, Mosienko skated into position. There was Bodnar again with another perfect pass. The Chicago player faked a defenseman out of position and blasted a long shot at the befuddled goalie, who stood helpless as the puck passed by him into the net for Mosienko's third score! This trio of tallies took all of 21 seconds—a record that is likely to hold for many a year.

Mosienko was done for the night, but his teammates were not. Infused with new life, they scored still another two goals against their now fog-eyed opponents to win an amazing 7 to 6 victory.

Source: *The National Hockey League Guide; 1967; page 78.*

1952 Seven Turnesa brothers become golf stars

Phenomenal! That's the only word that can describe the fact that all seven brothers of the Turnesa family, who were born and reared in Elmsford, N. Y., became outstanding golfers. Mike Turnesa was a greenskeeper at

Fairview Country Club in Elmsford, and he started his kids in the game. They learned fast.

Six of the boys—Mike, Jr., Frank, Joe, Phil, Doug and Jim —became professionals. The only Turnesa who didn't turn pro was Willie, the youngest. But he, too, was a superb golfer. Willie won the U. S. Amateur in 1938, and again in 1948; and he won the British Amateur in 1947.

Among them, the seven Turnesa brothers won a host of tournaments, and in 1952, Jim won the Professional Golfers Association championship.

Source: "Golf: Its History, People & Events"; Will Grimsley; Prentice-Hall, Inc.; 1966.

1953 Searls saws through a 32-inch log in 86.4 seconds

On November 5, 1953, during the Pacific Logging Congress held in the Civic Auditorium of Seattle, Washington, 46-year-old Paul Searls, a lumberjack, grabbed a seven-foot

bucking saw, and working furiously, cut through a log that was 32 inches in girth—in one minute and 26.4 seconds. Paul was six feet 3½ inches tall, and weighed 230 pounds at the time.

Source: *The Seattle Times; November 13, 1968; page 14, column 1.*

1953 Hillary and Norkay climb Mount Everest

Until Edmund Hillary, a New Zealand beekeeper, and
Tenzing Norkay, a Sherpa guide, native of the Himalayas,
conquered Mt. Everest in 1953, no fewer than ten other
teams had tried to scale the heights, and had failed. The
famed George Mallory lost his life in the attempt; so did a
party of Russian explorers lose theirs. The closest anyone
ever got to the summit was a Swiss group who, about a year
earlier, led by the same Tenzing Norkay, got within 1,000
feet of the goal.

Mount Everest towers 29,028 feet above sea level—about
five and one-half miles high in the sky—the tallest mountain
peak in the world. It is the last awful 1,000 feet of that
mountain that offers such a formidable challenge.

When climbers reach that height, the rarefied air takes
its toll. Because breathing is so difficult five miles above sea
level, a climber must work fast. He can carry only a certain
amount of oxygen on his back, and when that oxygen supply
is exhausted, he will be in dire peril. Because a climber must
work fast, the stint is fearfully exhausting. Moreover,
because things must be done with such dispatch, it is likely
that mistakes will be made.

Besides, a climber who essays Everest is burdened with
equipment, provisions, climbing gear, heavy clothes for
protection against frigid weather, and on top of all that, an
oxygen tank.

Near the summit of Everest, the winds bite bitterly in a

temperature that ranges between 30 and 40 degrees below zero. It was at this point—1,000 feet below the summit — that Hillary and Norkay took leave of their 12-man British team. They would now proceed by themselves to conquer the mountain.

On May 28, 1953, each loaded with a thirty-pound oxygen tank on his back, they began the last and most crucial lap. As they went up higher and higher, the conditions became worse; the cold was such that icicles clung to their masks. The last 40-foot ridge took the two men two and one-half hours. Hillary said later, "It was more like a lifetime."

Finally they reached the summit; and from there, great stretches of the world lay before them in all directions. On top of Mount Everest, they planted the flags of Nepal, India, and Great Britain, as well as the emblem of the United Nations.

The word didn't reach England until a few days later—on the eve of Queen Elizabeth's coronation. Seven weeks later, the young queen made Hillary a knight of the British Empire.

Source: "The Conquest of Everest"; Sir John Hunt; Dutton; 1954.

1953 Worsham hits a 104-yard wedge shot that is worth $62,000

The occasion was the 1953 world's championship tournament held on the Tam O'Shanter golf course in Chicago. Charley Harper had completed his final round with a birdie 3, and wound up the 72-hole tournament with a sparkling 279. Television cameras were focused on Charley as the likely winner, and fans swarmed over him seeking his autograph or some small souvenir. He looked like a sure thing.

Worsham and his two playing partners, who were striding down the fairway of the 18th hole, were nearly forgotten. From the last tee, Lew had hit an excellent drive which traveled neatly down the middle of the fairway and came to a halt a little over 100 yards from the pin. That shot brought his score up to 277. If he parred the par-four hole, which seemed to be likely for a golfer of his stature,

Worsham would wind up in second place with a 280 score. If he made what looked to be an exceptionally tough birdie, he would be locked in a tie with Harper.

But Worsham did the impossible. With an effortless swing, he lifted the ball over a small brook that guarded the green. The ball landed 25 feet from the pin, took a meek bounce, cleared a slight ridge, and rolled straight ahead into the cup!

The spectators went wild. Worsham's eagle-deuce had won the championship and the $25,000 first prize. Will Grimsley of the Associated Press called Worsham's eagle one of the ten greatest golf shots of all time. Officials measured the exact distance. It was 104 yards.

The tournament contract provided that the winner be paid $1,000 for each in a series of exhibitions. Worsham took part in 37 of these shows. Combined with his $25,000 first prize, that great shot was worth $62,000 to him.

Source: "Golf: Its History, People and Events"; Will Grimsley; Prentice Hall, Inc.; 1966; pages 290-91.

1954 Van den Berg skates 120 miles in seven and a half hours

Ice skating is the favorite winter sport in the Dutch province of Friesland, which since the 18th century has put on the world's longest and most difficult ice skating race.

This race is known as the *Elfstedentocht* ("Eleven Towns

Course"), so called because it is skated along the canals, rivers, and lakes connecting the 11 main towns of Friesland. The distance falls just short of 200 kilometers (approximately 124 miles), and the exact course varies somewhat from year to year, depending on ice conditions.

For the *Elfstedentocht* of February 3, 1954, all Dutch soldiers who wanted to skate in the race were given two days leave and free transportation to Leeuwarden, which serves as both starting and finishing point. Even the Dutch Parliament closed down for the day, since one of its most important members announced that he was going to participate.

All told, the 1954 *Elfstedentocht* attracted 138 formal contenders. In addition, as has always been the custom, there were several thousand other skaters who came out to skate the full distance at a more leisurely pace, without any thought of competing.

The winner of this ice-skating marathon was a young schoolteacher from the town of Nijbeets in Friesland, one Jeen van den Berg, who at the time was 26 years old. He covered the 124-mile distance in 7 hours 35 minutes, besting the previous record for the grueling course by more than an hour, and becoming a national hero in the process.

Source: New York Times; February 4, 1954; page 3 column 2. Letter from
J. B. Braaksma; Counselor for Cultural Affairs; Royal Netherlands
Embassy, Washington, D. C.

1954 Perry climbs a 20-foot rope in less than three seconds

In official rope climbing competitions, the athlete must lift himself up using only his hands. The competitor's feet must at no time be wound around the rope. This is a sport that requires enormous strength.

On April 3, 1954, pulling himself upward hand over hand, Don Perry of the University of California, Los Angeles, competing in the National Collegiate Athletic Association meet at Champaign, Illinois, climbed to the top of a 20-foot rope in 2.8 seconds—a world's record to be sure!

Source: *Chicago Tribune; April 4, 1954; Part 2, page 6, column 8.*

1954 Browning somersaults seven feet and three inches

In 1954, the world's record for the high jump was six feet, eleven and one-half inches, held by Walt Davis who was almost that tall himself. But that year there was a little five-foot nine-inch gymnast who could leap even higher.

Dick Browning, a 20-year-old sophomore of the University of Illinois, was generally acknowledged to be the world's greatest tumbler at the time. His execution of the somersault was nonpareil. He was so good he could beat the best high jumper of his day.

On April 27, 1954, at an exhibition in Santa Barbara, California, Dick Browning, rounding off his routine, somersaulted over a bar which was seven feet, three inches high. When Browning's record was reported, track coaches all over the country scoffed. Track rules specifically insist that a high jump be executed from a one-foot take-off. If this five-foot nine-inch midget did in fact leap seven feet, then he must have, they claimed, pushed off with two feet. However, all who had been present and carefully watched the performance avowed that when Browning took off, he had turned his body slightly in order to get more spring, and that, in fact, one of his feet left the ground before the other. Dick's leap, witnesses insisted, complied with all the rules.

Whether the jump was or was not according to Hoyle is really beside the point. For the wonder still stands: how could a man execute a somersault so high that he indeed did clear a seven-foot three-inch bar?

Source: *Letter from Charles M. Bellatti, Sports Information Director, University of Illinois; May 15, 1968.*

1954 Stapp travels 632 miles an hour in a rocket sled

In 1954, at Holloman Air Force Base Development Center at Alamogordo, the United States Air Force was conducting a series of experiments to test man's ability to withstand pressure. The Air Force had devised a contraption called a *Rocket Sled,* a jet engine bolted onto a platform mounted on steel wheels which was to run on rails. The vehicle, impelled by nine rockets with a total thrust of 40,000 pounds, weighed 2,000 pounds. The idea was to get the darned thing moving as fast as possible, and then have the rider brake it to a sudden halt. What effect would such a precipitous stop have upon the man in the sled?

On December 10, 1954, Lt. Col. John Stapp, then 44,

buckled on a plastic helmet, harnessed himself in place, and then zoomed off over the sands of New Mexico from a standing start. The acceleration was astonishing. Within only five seconds and within 2,800 feet, Stapp had reached a speed of 632 miles per hour. The Lieutenant Colonel stayed at that speed for merely half a second, and then put on the brakes. It took only one and one-half seconds for the rocket sled to grind to a complete halt. The pressure on Stapp was equal to 35 times his own body weight, and he blacked out. But only for a trice. At the moment of deceleration, he suffered intense pain, which passed very quickly. He had proven just how much the human body can take, and in the process he had moved over terra firma faster than any other human has done before or since.

During the experiment, Stapp survived a force of 22g; the normal limit is 12g.

Source: United Press International dispatch; December 27, 1954.

1954 Etchbaster, at age 60, becomes world's oldest athletic champion

Pierre Etchbaster, a spunky Basque from St. Jean de Luz in the French Pyrenees, has the distinction of being the oldest man ever to hold an international athletic championship.

In May 1928, he became the world's indoor court tennis champion. Played with bat, ball, and net in a four-walled cement court measuring 110 feet by 38 feet, this predecessor of lawn tennis goes back to the Middle Ages. In the 27 years between 1928 and 1954, Etchbaster, representing the Racquet & Tennis Club of New York, defended his title against all comers; and in every match he was victorious, often defeating men 20 years younger.

In 1954, when he reached the age of 60 years, Etchbaster, still undefeated, voluntarily stepped down.

Since then, Etchbaster has taught tennis and given exhibitions. His statue stands in the National Lawn Tennis Association Hall of Fame and Tennis Museum in Newport, Rhode Island.

Source: New York Times; February 24, 1955; page 30, column 2; February 25, 1955; page 25, column 3.

1955 Allen pitches 187 ringers out of 200 throws

Nobody could pitch horseshoes like Ted Allen. After he took up the game in 1921, he dominated all major tournaments for half a century. In the middle 1950's, Allen—who hailed from Boulder, Colorado—practically rewrote the record book.

To qualify for the 1955 World Horseshoe Pitchers Championship, he threw 200 horseshoes, wrapping 187 of the two-pound missiles around the ring. His average was a fat 93.5%. Neophytes, who squeal with delight when they get

one or two ringers in an entire game, will appreciate the drama of Allen's performance at Murray, Utah.

On July 26, 1955, Ted Allen, tied in a competition, threw double ringers 36 times in a row, a record of 72 consecutive perfect pitches. Of course, he won the world's title.

Source: "The Story of Horseshoes"; Ottie W. Reno; Vantage
Press; 1963; pages 167–69.

1955 Marciano knocks out 43rd man in 49 fights

Rocky Marciano, the blockbuster from Brockton, Mass., compiled the finest record of any professional heavyweight. He fought 49 times and won every bout.

Although a half-dozen or so fighters in the annals of boxing have completed their careers undefeated, no one stands on a pedestal as high as Rocky. For Marciano achieved the highest knockout record in the history of the sport—winning 43 of his bouts by a knockout.

A small heavyweight—standing but five feet 11 inches tall and weighing only 184—Marciano began his professional career in 1947. He promptly racked up 16 straight knockouts, only one of his opponents getting past the third round.

On September 23, 1952, Marciano fought Jersey Joe Walcott for the heavyweight championship of the world. Pounding his opponent mercilessly on the arms and body, Marciano wore Walcott down, and in the 13th round lowered the champ to the floor.

Marciano retained the world's heavyweight championship until he retired undefeated in 1955.

Source: "Ring Record Book"; Nat Fleischer; Ring Book Shop; 1967; page 736.

1956 Mosconi beats Moore in pocket billiards by running the entire game in one inning

On April 17, 1956, Willie Mosconi of Philadelphia was matched against Jimmy Moore of Albuquerque, New Mexico, in the world's pocket billiard tournament, held in Kingston, North Carolina. The game, held in front of 350 spectators at the Shamrock Billiard Center, began with Moore taking the table. The game was set at 150 points, which meant the first player to pocket 150 balls won. Moore played a safety on his first shot and never got another chance to show his skill, for the wizard of the green baize just ran out the entire game without a stop.

For those who had followed Willie's career, this wasn't too surprising. In Springfield, Ohio, in an exhibition match played in 1954 against a local hotshot, Mosconi established a world's record by running off 526 balls in a row, a little better than 37 racks. Willie, pitted against Luther Lassiter in San Francisco in March, 1953, in a world's championship match, won in only two innings.

Source: New York Times; April 18, 1956; page 35, column 3.

1956 Heckmann rides seven winners in one day

It was October 1, 1956, and the race track fraternity had gathered in goodly numbers at Hawthorne, Chicago's track for thoroughbreds. It was a day to remember.

Johnny Heckmann, a 24-year-old jockey, won the first race. When he followed by winning the second, it seemed that this was the young lad's lucky day. Heckmann stayed out of the third race, only because he didn't have a mount.

However, he got back on the track in the fourth race, and again he won. In the fifth, he failed to even as much as place. Nevertheless, three winners out of four seemed pretty good to the rail birds who started buzzing — especially since Heckmann's first two mounts yielded a daily-double that amounted to getting $141.20 for a $2.00 ticket. And it was a matter of comment that Heckmann's initial winner was a horse by the name of *Brandy's Last*.

And when, in the sixth race, Johnny Heckmann brought home *Letmego* to win $4,000, the excitement mounted. In the seventh, Johnny led *My Preference* to the tape, winning another $5,000, and the 12,000 track fans, at first dumbfounded, became hysterical. This jockey was really hot — no question about that — and it seemed that almost every horseplayer on the scene flocked to the windows to put his money down on Heckmann.

Heckmann didn't disappoint them. In the eighth race, in a grueling finish, Johnny drove *Royal Monarch* over the finish line to win by a neck. Heckmann had now brought in six winners in one afternoon.

In the ninth Johnny was atop *Dawney*, the favorite. This turned out to be an extremely tight run, yet the incredible man brought *Dawney* home by a head. Heckmann had made history, winning seven races in one afternoon! But his streak had not yet burned itself out. On the following day, Johnny won two out of the three races he entered.

Source: Chicago Tribune; October 2, 1956; Part 4, page 1, column 4.

1956 Larsen pitches a perfect game in the World Series

The date was October 8, 1956. The New York Yankees were locked in a struggle with the Brooklyn Dodgers, a team reputed to have the greatest hitters ever assembled. There were Roy Campanella, the famous catcher, and Duke Snider, the famous slugger, and Gil Hodges, and Pee Wee Reese and Jackie Robinson. Two of these stars have been enshrined

in baseball's Hall of Fame, and the other three are destined for similar immortality.

Facing this phalanx of explosive offense, any pitcher would be somewhat cowed. But not Don Larsen. Mixing his fast ball with a slow curve and a tricky slider, Larsen baffled the Dodger stalwarts, mowing them down inning after inning in one-two-three order. Not one of the Dodgers' 27 batters reached first base. By the end of the afternoon, the Yanks had held on to a 2-0 lead, as their 6-foot, 4-inch pitcher completed the first—and the only—perfectly pitched baseball game in World Series history.

Source: *New York Times;* October 9, 1956; page 1, column 2.

1957 Barker wins a professional boxing match in less than seven seconds

The opening bell had hardly stopped ringing when Bob Roberts of Nigeria rushed toward his English opponent, Teddy Barker, in a bout of welterweights held at Maestag, Wales, on September 2, 1957. Mr. Roberts was extremely eager to get the first punch, so eager that he hauled off with a wild right overhand. Barker ducked under the punch and came through with a right counter, a sharp jab that caught the overenthusiastic Roberts square on the jaw.

The Nigerian collapsed, but climbed to his feet before the count began. However, the referee saw that glazed look in the fallen man's eyes. To save Roberts from further punishment, he halted the fight before either man could swing again, awarding the victory to Barker on a technical knockout. The whole thing had taken less than seven seconds. It was the shortest bout on record.

Source: "Ring Record Book"; Nat Fleischer; The Ring Book Shop; 1967; page 740.

1957 Anderson lifts 6,270 pounds of dead weight with his back

In his early 20's, Paul Anderson of Toccoa, Georgia ranged in weight from 300 pounds to 360 pounds. Not only was he one of the biggest men around, but he was unquestionably the strongest man on earth. The powerful 5-foot, 10-inch Georgian had wrists that measured nine inches around. His neck was a burly 23 inches in circumference.

Anderson was the first man in history who could press, as the weight lifters say it (that is, lift from the floor to above his head), a barbell of 400 pounds. Among other feats, Paul could do three knee bends in succession while he carried a 900-pound barbell across his shoulders. He powered his way to an Olympic championship as an amateur.

On June 12, 1957, Paul Anderson, then a professional weight lifter, established himself as the superman of the age. He placed a steel safe full of lead on a specially-made table, and then loaded the remaining surface with bars of heavy auto parts. He then crawled under the table and placed his hands on a stool to support himself. Then, elevating his back, he lifted the table inches off the floor—a weight of 6,270 pounds!

Three tons is just about the weight of two good-sized automobiles. Or to put it another way, Anderson lifted the combined weight of all the players on a 33-man college football team.

Source: "The Encyclopedia of Sports"; Frank G. Menke; A. S. Barnes; 1963; page 1004.

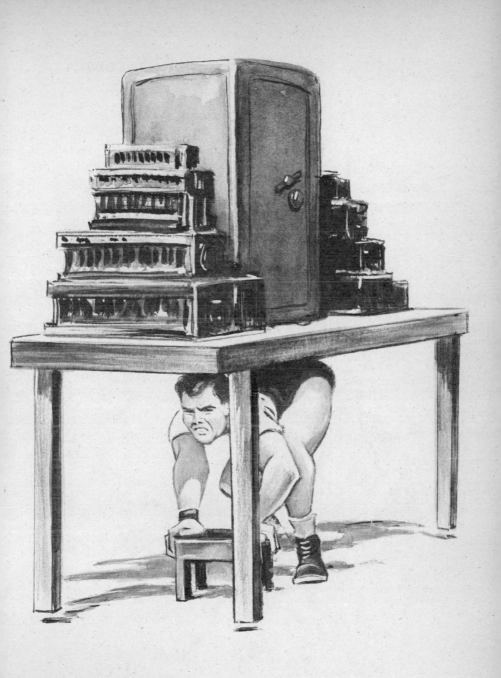

1959 Shoulders wins his 16th rodeo championship

The modern rodeo program includes many events and specialty numbers—such as trick riding, fancy roping, and clowns—that would have amazed the men who originated the

sport a century ago in the rough cowtowns of the frontier. But the five main rodeo events—saddle bronc riding, bareback riding, calf roping, bull riding, and steer wrestling—are the same today as they were at the beginning of the sport, and these are the contests that attract the most daring and skilled of the new breed of professional riders.

The all-time champion rodeo man, now retired from active competition and running a ranch in Henryetta, Oklahoma, is Jim Shoulders. Ironically, he was a born-and-bred city boy, the son of an automobile mechanic in Tulsa.

Shoulders, who has been described as the finest rider in the history of the West, specialized in bareback and bull riding. He won his first rodeo competition at the age of 14. In 1946, when he graduated from high school, he turned pro. Just three years later, he accumulated winnings of $21,495 and thus earned rodeo's most coveted title of "All-around Cowboy."

In the seasons that followed, Jim Shoulders was world bull-riding champion seven times and world bareback-riding champion four times, won the all-around cowboy title four more times (1956–1959), and was a runner-up for it on four other occasions.

Since his retirement, the bareback and all-around cowboy records set by Shoulders have been tied, but no rodeo rider has ever come near accumulating as many titles.

Source: Rodeo Sports News, 1972; pages 77, 125–131. Letters from Randy Witte, Executive Director, Rodeo Information Foundation.

1959 Foster stays under water for over 13 minutes

On March 15, 1959, Robert Foster entered the swimming pool of the Bermuda Palms Hotel in San Rafael, California. Before entering the pool, Foster had primed himself for his ordeal by breathing in oxygen from a tank for a half hour.

As Foster lowered himself into the pool, members of the Marine Skin Divers Club prepared to time him. A doctor was present and an expert in first aid stood by, for Foster intended to stay at the bottom of that pool longer than any other man had ever been under water.

This he did. When he emerged, the clockers stopped their watches at 13 minutes, 42.5 seconds.

Source: San Francisco Chronicle; March 16, 1959; page 6, column 2.

1959 Sharman drops in 56 consecutive foul shots in pro basketball

On March 18, 1959, Bill Sharman began putting together a string of free throws that would make basketball history. On April 9th, when his string ended, the star guard of the world-champion Boston Celtics had dropped in 56 foul shots in a row, a record performance.

In some games, Bill would step to the foul line only once; in other games, he would sink as many as eight out of eight tries.

In that same season Bill established an all-time record for foul shooting by connecting with 93.2% of his one-handed push shots from the foul line.

Source: "Sharman on Basketball Shooting"; Bill Sharman; Prentice-Hall, Inc.; 1965; page 87.
New York Times; April 10, 1959; page 35, column 1.

1959 Dean lands a 2,664-pound shark with a hook and rod

Fishermen notoriously are prone to exaggerate—a pound here, a foot there. But the Alf Dean story that came out of Southern Australia on April 21, 1959—well, it was just too big *not* to be true.

Dean, a well-known game fisherman in his late 50's, had hooked into a 2,664-pound white shark near Ceduna, South Australia. It was the largest fish ever landed by hook and rod. The monster, measured and verified by the International Game Fish Association, was 16 feet, 10 inches long, and measured 9 feet, 6 inches in girth.

Source: *Letter from International Game Fish Association; Marion McKelvey, Secretary; April 15, 1968.*

1959 Lubanski bowls two perfect games in a row

On June 22, 1959, Eddie Lubanski, a former professional baseball pitcher, was entered in the Mixed Scotch Doubles bowling tournament in Miami, Florida. Before a rapt audience, Lubanski rolled 12 straight strikes to fashion a perfect game. That was really nothing new for Lubanski, who once ruined a local television show which had offered $10,000 in cash to anybody who could bowl a perfect game. Lubanski turned the trick, collected the money, and put the show off the air.

However, in his second game, Ed continued to roll perfect shots. The crowd was agog and then sat completely electrified. For before he was through, Ed Lubanski had bowled 24 strikes in a row—two perfect games back to back in big-time competition!

Source: Britannica Book of the Year; 1960; page 115.

1960 Moloney and Evans walk from San Francisco to New York in 66 days

More than 3,000 miles separate the Golden Gate Bridge in San Francisco from the Coliseum on Columbus Circle in New York City. Most people who travel between these two points do it in just a few hours by jet airliner, but there are a few determined men and women who have made the grueling trip on foot.

The record for this transcontinental hike was, ironically, set by two men who were not even Americans: British Royal Air Force Sergeant Patrick Moloney of Limerick, Ireland, age 34, and British Royal Army Sergeant Mervyn Evans of Frefiw, Wales, age 33.

Accompanied by a third British soldier, who followed them in a jeep hauling a trailer in which they slept each night, Moloney and Evans set out from San Francisco on April 13, 1960. Every day thereafter, beginning at five in the morning and continuing until eight at night, Moloney and Evans marched in army route-step cadence, striding steadily eastward along a seemingless endless ribbon of concrete.

Passing through 11 states, they averaged 46 miles a day. They encountered adverse weather conditions of all kinds, and crossed a diversity of terrain that included the deserts of Nevada, the Rocky Mountains, the plains of the Midwest, and the rugged hills of southwestern Pennsylvania. All along the way, they were spot-checked by American Legion observers, who had been asked by the British War Office to make sure that the two intrepid hikers walked the full distance without accepting any ride.

Though occasionally bothered by blisters, nausea, and melancholy, Moloney and Evans doggedly stuck to their guns, each wearing out two pairs of boot heels during their journey. Moloney lost two pounds en route; Evans, four.

Tanned and weatherbeaten but still in peak physical condition, Moloney and Evans reached New York City on June 17, 1960. They had beaten the existing west-east transcontinental record by about six days, covering the 3,022-mile distance in 66 days, 4 hours, and 17 minutes.

Source: New York Times; April 7, 1960; page 37, column 3; April 13, 1960; page 19, column 3; June 18, 1960; page 25, column 2.

1960 Kittinger drops 16 miles before opening his parachute

Inscribed on the cockpit door of the balloon
was a legend that read: "The world's biggest step."
And indeed it was! For the balloon carrying Joseph
Kittinger, a United States Air Force captain, was 19 miles
up in the sky, sailing along at a height of 102,000 feet over
New Mexico, when on August 16, 1960, Kittinger took that
step, and made history.

Falling freely through the air, Kittinger picked up speed
each second. Mile after mile he fell, with his parachute firmly
packed on his back. But though he encountered a pitiless
wind as he reached a falling speed of over 600 miles an
hour, the 32-year-old Kittinger maintained his composure.
It wasn't easy to brook a temperature as low, at times, as
94 degrees below zero.

Yet, before releasing his chute, the dauntless captain
dropped 84,700 feet—more than 16 miles! He had fallen
through space for four minutes and 38 seconds, a world's
record for a free fall.

After Kittinger opened his parachute, it took 13 minutes
for him to float down the last three miles to terra firma.

Source: "Parachuting Complete"; William Saunders; Para Press; 1966; pages
56–57.

1961 Abertondo swims the English Channel round trip

The English Channel has been licked by such as legion of athletes that today the feat of swimming its treacherous 22 miles is old hat. But the particular Channel feat of Antonio Abertondo, though dreamed of for decades by swimmers, had never been achieved before.

When on September 21, 1961, Abertondo waded into the chilly sea off Dover, he had set himself an unprecedented challenge: he would swim not only from Dover to Calais, France, but—without a break—from Calais back to Dover—a round trip, without rest, of 44 miles!

The Argentine, then 42 years old and a hefty man with a trace of middle-age spread, and greased from head to toe to protect himself against the cold, entered the water in the morning. Abertondo negotiated the first half of the trip in 18 hours and 50 minutes. Ashore in France, he paused for two minutes—only long enough to sip a hot drink. Then he plunged once again into the tide-tossed waters.

After a few miles, weariness set in — extreme weariness. On the return trip, the waves hit harder, belting his face until it swelled. Even under the goggles his eyes grew sore. Hallucinations followed, the swimmer imagining that huge sharks were in his path.

But Abertondo pumped on, arm over arm and kick after kick; and yard by yard he put the miles behind him.

It was more than a day since he had last touched land—a full 24 hours and 25 minutes after he had left Calais—and 43 hours and 15 minutes after he entered the water at

Dover—that Antonio Abertondo writhed out of the surf onto the English shore. The last mile had taken a full two hours. Then, like an agonized shipwreck, he collapsed in the arms of his astounded observers.

Source: *The Times of London; September 23, 1961; page 8, column 5.*

1962 Chamberlain scores 100 points in a professional basketball game

It figured to be a no account game in a no account place. Neither the New York Knickerbockers nor the Philadelphia Warriors were going anywhere in the National Basketball Association standings in 1962, and the neutral site where they played, the little Hershey Arena in Hershey, Pennsylvania, was well off the major league road map.

But on the night of March 2, Wilt Chamberlain made basketball history. Standing 7-feet, 1-inch, Wilt the Stilt heaved 100 points into the basket! In compiling his score, the perfectly coordinated giant scored on 36 field goals in 63 tries, and sank 28 out of 32 free throws. Since that day, no one has come close to Chamberlain's record—not even Wilt himself.

Needless to say, his team won, 169 to 147.

Source: New York Times; March 3, 1962; page 14, column 1.

1962 Patricia Barnett roller-skates more than 20 miles in one hour

Pat Barnett, a trim, good-looking English secretary, lives in North London with her husband, two dogs, and two cats. At one time or another, she has broken every women's roller-skating record from two miles to 201 miles. Moreover, her time for the 10-mile course was 12 seconds faster than that of the British men's roller-skating champ. All told, Pat Barnett has won 15 world roller-skating titles and 27 British titles.

On June 24, 1962, Pat Barnett set her most outstanding speed-skating record at the Brixton Skating rink in London. During a period of one hour, she covered a distance of 20 miles and 1,355 yards—the greatest distance ever skated by a woman in that time.

Source: The Sun (London); February 6, 1971.

1962   Baldasare swims the English Channel under water

Swimming the English Channel even under the best of conditions is an arduous and challenging feat, but the self-imposed handicap of Fred Baldasare had never been overcome before: the 44-year-old frogman from Cocoa Beach, Florida, swam from France to England *under water*.

Fred had assayed the feat twice before, and had failed. When on July 11, 1962, he strapped on his rubber suit and his oxygen tank, he well knew what to expect. Under the water, a swimmer has no sense of direction. So to avoid straying off course, Baldasare swam behind a towed cage.

Baldasare also knew that the currents underneath the surface are more powerful than those on the surface. For that hazard, there was no solution.

Swimming in the bowels of the Channel, Baldasare was swept by a strong tide far to the north of the course he had laid out, much farther north than any other Channel swimmer had ever been. It is estimated that he traveled nearly twice the 22 miles of the Channel span.

Nevertheless, 18 hours and one minute after he had submerged off the coast of France, he surfaced near the greens of the Royal Cinque Golf Course in Kent — a nonpareil human submarine.

Source: *The World Almanac; 1965; page 888.*
The Times of London; July 12, 1962; page 10, column 3.

1962 Blancas shoots 18 holes of golf in 55 strokes

The finest round of golf ever played in tournament competition was registered on August 19, 1962, by Homero Blancas who completed the 5,002-yard Premier Golf Course in Longview, Texas, with a round of 17 under par.

At the time, Blancas was just 24 years old, a recent University of Houston graduate. Playing in the first round of the Premier Invitational tournament, Blancas covered the nine holes in 27, then came back in 28. Playing consistently as well as brilliantly, Homero recorded 13 birdies and one eagle.

Up till then, the existing U.S. record was 59, held jointly by Sam Snead and Earl Fry.

Blancas won the trophy with a score of 256 for the 72 holes, an average of 64 per round.

Source: New York Times; August 21, 1962; page 41, column 3.

 **The Wallendas form a human pyramid on the high wires for the last time**

According to veteran ringmaster Fred Bradna, the most exciting circus act ever offered was the high-wire act of a German troupe who dubbed themselves "The Great Wallendas." The moniker was entirely justified.

Defying death, the Wallendas would ride bicycles on high wires which extended 70 feet above the circus floor, and they rode without a safety net below them.

In 1928, in their debut at Madison Square Garden in New York City, the Wallendas sought to outdo themselves. They announced they would form a human pyramid while riding on bicycles over a high wire.

Joseph and Herman Wallenda pedaled two bikes over two parallel wires. A pole connected the two riders. The

pole extended from the back of Joseph to the chest
of Herman.

On this pole, Karl Wallenda had balanced a chair, and
he nonchalantly sat down on the chair while the other
two Wallendas pedaled along. And to cap the climax, the
96-pound Helen Kries Wallenda stood on Karl's shoulders
with arms outstretched and a big smile on her face.

As the Wallendas pedaled across the high wires, the
crowd was glued in fearsome awe. A little slip and all would
crash to eternal rest, for there was no safety net spread
below them. When the performers successfully traversed

the distance, the crowd first caught its breath, and then broke into a tremendous cheer that lasted for 15 minutes. Circus historians couldn't recall such a reception ever.

But if the Wallendas performed brilliantly, it was due to constant practice and painstaking care. They went about their work with Teutonic precision. First, Herman would march into the arena with his thermometer, followed by the other Wallendas to measure wind, humidity, or anything else that might affect the stars of the high wires. Above all, the Wallendas were confident artists. Herman once did a back flip on the high wire — typically without a net!

But unfortunately, this nonpareil stunt of the Wallendas was too high-pressure and too exacting for them to forever avoid the slight flaw that would mean disaster. In 1962, before a crowd of 6,000 in Detroit, the pyramid gave in 36 feet above the floor. Two of The Great Wallendas fell to their deaths. Another was critically injured.

Bravely, the Wallendas performed again *on the following night*. But the act was never the same again; and the troupe broke up in 1968.

Source: "The Big Top"; Fred Bradna; Simon and Schuster; 1952; pages 264-270.

1963 Clark wins seven Grand Prix races in one year

In auto racing, skill, luck, and fuel mixture are all prime ingredients. Jim Clark had all of these going for him in 1963. This was only his third full season of racing, but Jim came through with the finest record any driver has ever had. The handsome Scot scored seven victories out of 10 Grand Prix races.

In that one year, Clark, just 27 at the time, won, in order, the Grand Prix of Belgium, The Netherlands, France, Great Britain, Italy, Mexico, and South Africa. In the other three championships which Jim entered he made a strong showing. He was well in front in Monaco, with three-quarters of the race completed, when his engine broke down. In the German Grand Prix, he came in second. In the U. S. leg of this prestigious circuit, Clark's batteries died at the start. Jim pushed his car back to the pits, installed a new battery, and then drove so brilliantly that he finished third despite his crippling late start.

Entering a completely different type of race that same year, the Indianapolis 500, Clark came in second, trailing the winner by a mere 34 seconds—a startling performance by an Indy rookie.

For the year, Clark won 19 out of the 30 auto racing events of all categories he entered.

The astounding quality of this performance can be measured only when it is considered that in racing in a Grand Prix a driver must be able to shift gears just about every two seconds in order to negotiate the winding roads,

and that he must be equally adept at taking corners and
in accelerating to speeds up to 200 miles an hour in just
a flash.

Before he died in a racing crash, in 1968 at age 32,
Jim Clark had won 25 Grand Prix victories. Just two years
after his debut at Indianapolis, the fabulous Scotchman
became the first foreigner in nearly 50 years to win that
great classic.

Source: *New York Times; April 8, 1968; page 1, column 3.*
*"Jim Clark: Portrait of a Great Driver"; Graham Gauld in collaboration
with others; Hamlyn Publishing Group, Ltd.; 1968.*

1964 Bosher shears 565 sheep in one work day

In Australia and New Zealand, the ability to shear sheep quickly means income, since a shearer is generally paid on a piece-work basis. A champion shearer is also somewhat of a hero among his fellow workers, and shearing competitions are regularly held.

On April 13, 1964, Colin Bosher proved himself to be the fastest shearer who ever lived. The 31-year-old native of Te Awamutu began trimming in the morning, and up to noon his machine clipped away at a rate of better than one ewe per 50 seconds. Though quite exhausted and hungry, he kept to his task without let-up or surcease for eight hours and 53 minutes. By the end of the work day, Bosher had shorn 565 Romney and Perendale ewes at the average rate of one each 56 seconds—a record of 565 sheep within a single 9-hour working day. Bosher didn't stop his chores seven minutes early by choice — he simply ran out of sheep.

Source: *The Weekly News, Auckland, New Zealand; April 22, 1964; page 58, column 3.*

1964 Parker glides continuously in the air for 644 miles

On July 31, 1964, Al Parker, a 45-year-old glider veteran picked up a couple of candy bars and a quart of water, and headed for the Odessa, Texas, airport.

At 9:45 a.m., he climbed into a slick Sisu A-1 sailplane and was towed 2,000 feet above the ground by a motorized plane. Parker headed due north and then detached his craft, gaining altitude by using the upcurrents under the clouds. He was abetted by a tail wind of 25 miles per hour.

As he crossed the Oklahoma panhandle, Parker swooped up and down at altitudes of 3,000 to 5,000 feet. Over Colorado, he ran into a thunderstorm; but Parker climbed over some of the clouds and penetrated through others until he spotted a small airport in Kimball, Nebraska, where he landed. He had traveled 644 miles in the air without a motor, at an average speed of 61 miles an hour, during a flight of ten and one-half hours.

Source: Soaring *Magazine*; August, 1964; page 7.

1964 Lenore Modell, age 14, swims the English Channel

Thirty-eight years had passed since the English Channel had first been conquered by a woman. When Lenore Modell, a young slip of a girl, got around to the job on September 3, 1964, a dozen other females had negotiated the perilous swim. Hours after Lenore took off from Gris Nez, France, a large crowd gathered on the cliffs of Dover to accord Miss Modell a specially enthusiastic acclamation—for Lenore was only five months past her 14th birthday —the youngest swimmer to ever conquer the Channel. Her time was 15 hours, 27 minutes.

Lenore Modell was one of those miraculous teen-age water babies from California, who rewrote the record books in the early 1960's. The California coaches had learned that during training they could arouse teen-agers to unbelievable aspirations. Lenore had practiced day after day, for hours at a time. The day came when she tried the Channel.

As she neared land, her exuberance was so great that the little miss almost swam up Dover Harbor by mistake. But a tide carried her to her goal at South Foreland Point, where the waiting crowd cheered her lustily.

Source: *The Times of London; September 4, 1964; page 10, column 3.*

1964 Mickey Wright shoots a 62 in golf

On November 15, 1964, the Tall City Open on the sprawling 6,286-yard Hogan Park Golf Course at Midland, Texas, was coming to an end. In the first two rounds of this Ladies Professional Golf Associations tournament, Mickey Wright, whom some consider the finest woman golfer of all time, shot a 73 and a 72, leaving her 10 strokes off the lead. Her mediocre scores induced her to play a brash, daring game on the final Sunday. There was nothing to lose.

On the first hole, a 457-yard, par-5 dogleg, Mickey got off a fine drive. She then layed her second shot just 18 inches from the cup. It was an easy eagle-three.

She birdied the next three holes, then parred four more, and completed the first nine in an astounding 30, sinking putts of 15 and 25 feet.

Mickey carried the momentum into the second nine, and went through the last half in 32—winding up with a record-shattering 62. (The men's record for the same course was 66.)

It wasn't until the final hole, however, that Mickey even dreamed of winning the tournament. On No. 18, she cautiously two-putted for a par, and tied for first place. The tournament went into a play-off.

Mickey went back on the course, shot two straight birdies, and gained the victory.

Source: Sports Illustrated; November 23, 1964; pages 83-85.

1964 Cathie Connelly dances the twist for more than four days

For some people, social dancing is a serious competitive enterprise that calls for great physical endurance. Take the case of Mrs. Cathie Connelly (now Mrs. Harvey). In 1964 she was a 35-year-old widow and mother of three in Dundee, Scotland. As a youngster, Cathie developed her dancing muscles by doing the Highland Fling. While working in a factory in Dundee, just for a lark she entered a marathon twist contest. She did so well, though, that she began to take marathon dancing more seriously.

On Tuesday, November 24, 1964, at the Theatre Royal Ballroom in the northern England community of Tyldesley, Cathie set out to prove she could out-twist anyone in the world. During the four days that followed, she danced steadily, except for a five-minute break every hour and a 20-minute break every four hours.

Cathie didn't stop dancing until Saturday, by which time she had twisted for a total of 101 hours.

Source: Leigh, Tyldesley and Atherton Journal; December 3, 1964.

1965 Karen Muir sets a world's swimming record at age 12

When she was but nine, her parents sent little Karen Muir to her first swimming lessons; they hoped that the timid, freckle-faced child would gain some much needed confidence. Three years later, Karen, now 12, and a good swimmer, traveled to Blackpool, England, to compete in the British championships. It was August 11, 1965. She was going to compete against 17-year-old Linda Ludgrove, who had set a world's record just two weeks before in the backstroke.

In a preliminary heat of the 110-yard backstroke event in a Blackpool stadium, Karen started to churn through the waters at a brilliant pace. The timers gasped as they clocked her speed at one minute, 8.7 seconds, a world's record. Karen was the youngest athlete in history to hold a world's record in a major sporting event.

The phenomenal water baby went on to achieve three full victories in the English event, and was named star of the meet.

Source: Newsweek magazine; August 23, 1965; page 69.

1965 Manry sails across the Atlantic in a 13½-foot dinghy

A simple man, just a 47-year-old suburbanite living
in Willowick, near Cleveland, Ohio, Robert Manry held a snug
copy-editing job on the *Cleveland Plain Dealer*. One fine day,
Manry told his wife, "There comes a time when one must
decide about one's dreams — to risk everything to achieve
them, or to sit the rest of one's life in the backyard." Bob
had had a boyhood dream of sailing across the Atlantic all
by himself.

So Manry prepared *Tinkerbelle,* a 13½-foot racing dinghy,
for the adventure of his life. The 35-year-old sailboat had
cost him but $250, and Manry readied it on June 1, 1965,
with the object of departing from Falmouth, Massachusetts,
and sailing to Falmouth, England. He loaded his craft with a
three-month supply of high concentrate foods, 28 gallons of
water, and a harmonica. And he covered the boat and himself
with a $50,000 insurance policy.

Manry was seeking fulfillment and not publicity, and so he
didn't even give the staff of his own newspaper the story.
He simply asked for a leave of absence and told his editor,
"I'll be back at work at 5 o'clock on August 29." As it
turned out, the rival Cleveland newspaper got the story first.

En route, there were moments when it seemed that Manry
wouldn't be back to work at all. Five times he was washed
off the deck, only to be saved by a life line he had lashed
around his waist. On another occasion, not so stormy, he was
bowled off the deck, but luckily caught the rigging of his
dinghy as it sailed past him. For lack of Vitamin B, his

fingers and toes swelled and peeled; and after a month the ghostly hallucinations which bedevil lonely seamen set in. But his worst fear was that his tiny craft would be run over in the night by a larger ship. Seventy-eight days after he left port, Manry reached his destination to become a reluctant international hero. The return trip for him and his *Tinkerbelle* was not quite so harrowing: both were put aboard the *Queen Mary*, and took the voyage home showered with laurel, accolade, and all manner of comfort.

Source: Newsweek magazine; August 30, 1965; pages 37-38.

1965 McInnes stays aloft almost 12 hours on a kite

In the 1950's, water skiing came into its own. In the 1960's, the sport became so popular that it spawned an assortment of oddments: jumping over obstacles, riding barefoot, and a variety of acrobatic stunts.

On October 5, 1965, a 34-year-old carpet layer from Henderson, Kentucky, by the name of Dick McInnes, assembled a crew at Newburgh Dam on the Ohio River. He was out to make a record of sorts. Standing on skis, McInnes was towed along by an 18-foot Glasspar Sportsman, powered by a 150-horsepower Mercruiser inboard-outboard. As the Glasspar pulled McInnes along over the surface of the Ohio, Dick held fast to a huge kite, which he had sailing in the air. When he got up enough speed, McInnes slowly wafted into the air, and soon reached an altitude of 100 feet. Thus, towed by the boat and the kite, McInnes remained aloft for 11 hours and 59 minutes, covering a distance of approximately 390 miles!

During this long jaunt, the skiing-flyer had to drop down to the water just a few times in order to pass under the Ohio's bridges.

Dick had attached himself to the kite by a special harness he had built. When aloft, he maintained contact with his crew by means of a special telephone. En route, McInnes staved off hunger by nibbling from a container of diet food.

Surprisingly, the skiing-flyer suffered little discomfort other than cramped legs and hips.

Source: *The Water Skier;* December-January, 1966.
Letter from Dick McInnes; August 6, 1968.

1965 Linster does 6,006 consecutive push-ups without pause

On October 7, 1965, 16-year old Charles Linster of Wilmette, Illinois, got his coaches at New Trier High School to act as his witnesses. The young man, then five feet six and one-half inches tall and weighing 153 pounds, was going to attempt an endurance feat that would put his name into the record books.

Chick Linster, an accomplished gymnast, had done an awful lot of practicing doing push-ups. The push-up, a simple enough exercise in itself, consists of stretching out one's full length, chest down on the floor, and then, keeping a straight back, lifting one's self off the floor by pressing on the palms of the hands. The descent is made by simply bending the elbows until the chest touches the floor once again. This common exercise is seen in almost all gymnastic classes. A dozen push-ups is considered a fairly good workout for the average man who is in good physical condition.

On that day, performing for three hours and 54 minutes, Chick Linster executed 6,006 push-ups without stopping.

Source: Sports Illustrated; October 25, 1965; page 101. Letter from
R. W. Linster; December 9, 1968.

1965 Breedlove speeds an automobile at over 600 miles an hour

In 1963, Craig Breedlove of West Los Angeles, California drove his car for a land speed record of 400 miles per hour.

In 1964, Breedlove did 500 miles per hour.

On November 15, 1965, skimming over the Salt Flats of Bonneville, Utah, Craig Breedlove drove his jet car, *Spirit of America*, at the officially recognized speed of 601 miles per hour. He used five miles of track to build up his speed before entering the officially measured mile. After completing his first run, he turned back—for so the rules prescribed—

and initiated the return lap by starting five and one-half miles away from the measured mile.

P.S.: Lee Breedlove, his wife, drove her husband's car on November 4 and captured the woman's record. Her speed: a mere 308.56 miles per hour.

Source: New York Times; November 16, 1965; page 61, column 1.

1965 Le Bel jumps over 17 barrels on skates

The rules of jumping on skates are quite specific: the barrels must measure 16 inches in diameter and be 30 inches wide; the skater must clear the barrels cleanly without touching any one of them. Since the hazard of crashing is great, the barrels are made of a fibrous composition that has some give to it. Nevertheless, failing to jump over a barrel

at great speed involves danger to limb and neck. Only those of great courage and confidence essay this sport.

On December 18, 1965, Kenneth LeBel, a native of Lake Placid, New York, and Jacques Favero, a Canadian, met at the Grossinger Hotel in Liberty, New York, to compete in a match which would determine the world's champion barrel jumper. After Favero had catapulted himself over 16 barrels, the 180-pound LeBel circled the rink a couple of times to get up speed. Then he roared down the 200-foot straightaway, leaped, and sailed through the air at a speed of 40 miles an hour. LeBel had jumped over 17 barrels, darting through the air for a distance of 28 feet and 8 inches!

Source: Letter from Irv Jaffe; National Winter Sports Inc.; New York, N.Y.; April 8, 1968.

1966 Unser drives up Pike's Peak at better than a mile a minute

The Pike's Peak Auto Hill Climb, established in 1916, is one of America's most dangerous and challenging automobile races. Its 12.42-mile course has 230 curves, and a rise of 4,708 feet from start to finish.

On some relatively level stretches of the Colorado mountain road, contestants can open up to more than 100 miles per hour; but at other places, hairbreadth turns and sudden switchbacks make speeds in excess of 40 miles per hour mortally perilous. The slightest hesitation or error in judgment can send a car and its driver hurtling to destruction over the side of a steep, rugged cliff.

Not surprisingly, the Pike's Peak race has long attracted some of the finest racing drivers in America. Over the years, the roster of entrants has included such greats as Barney Oldfield, Eddie Rickenbacker, "Hughie" Hughes, Roy Stentz, Parnelli Jones, and Mario Andretti.

Most of all, though, the Pike's Peak Auto Hill Climb is associated with the Unser family of championship drivers. Louis Unser, affectionately known as the "Old Man of the Mountain," first entered the race in 1926; between 1936 and 1953, he was victorious nine times. His sons Jerry and Al have also won the grueling event.

But the all-time champion in the hill climb is another of Louis's sons: Robert W. "Bobby" Unser. The winner of the 1968 Indianapolis 500 and a world-renowned driver, Bobby Unser finished first in the Pike's Peak Auto Hill Climb 11 times in 14 years (1956–1969), a mark that will probably never be surpassed.

Moreover, Unser set the course record in each of the race's three main divisions. In 1969, he won the stock car event in the time of 13:04.05. In 1964, he won the sports car event in the time of 13:19.1. And in the championship division competition of 1966, Bobby Unser, driving a 336-cubic-inch Chevrolet, completed the race in an amazing 11:54.9—an average speed of better than 60 miles per hour on one of the roughest and most treacherous racing courses in the world!

Source: The official program of the Pike's Peak Auto Hill Climb.
New York Times Encyclopedic Almanac.

1966 Drake shoots an arrow more than 1,100 yards

Using longbows, the famed yeomen of medieval England prided themselves on their ability to shoot their cloth-yard arrows as far as 600 feet. This is an impressive figure, admittedly, but it cannot compare to the distance achieved by Barry Drake, a 20th-century flight-archer equipped with a footbow.

Designed especially for long-distance shooting, the footbow cannot be drawn In the usual vertical posture. Instead, the archer must strap it to his feet, then shoot it while lying flat on his back. He uses both his hands to draw the bowstring, and lifts his feet to give his arrow the best possible angle of elevation. The footbow's tensile resistance is two to three times that of a longbow.

With this unique instrument, Barry Drake, the world's most outstanding footbow archer, set a world distance record. In October 1966, in a National Archery Association sanctioned competition at Ivanpha Lake, California, Drake shot an arrow 1,100 yards and 1 inch—five and a half times farther than could Robin Hood at his best.

Source: Letter from Fred Schuette, Executive Secretary, American Archery Council.

1966 Cloninger, a pitcher, hits two grand-slam homers in one game

On July 3, 1966, Tony Cloninger was the nominee of the Atlanta Braves to pitch in Candlestick Park against the slugging San Francisco Giants. The young fireballer had won five of his previous six starts, and was fast making a name for himself as one of the most promising hurlers in the National League. But on this particular day, Cloninger was to make his name with the bat, a futile weapon in the hands of most hurlers.

Tony's teammates started pounding the ball in the top of the first inning and scored three runs. When Cloninger stepped to the plate with two outs, the bases were loaded with his Braves. Tony worked the count to three balls and two strikes, and then connected with a fastball and set it sailing over the center-field fence, more than 410 feet away.

Armored with a seven-run lead before throwing a single pitch, Cloninger breezed through the San Francisco batting order for the first three innings. When he came to bat in the top of the fourth, Cloninger again found the bags full of Braves—this time again with two out. And again Cloninger walloped the ball for a homer!

Before the day was over, the Atlanta pitcher drove in another run with a single. He had driven in nine of his team's runs in a 17–3 victory, and had become the first National Leaguer—and the first pitcher in either league—to hit two grand-slam home-runs in a single game.

Source: New York Times; July 4, 1966.

1966 Roelants runs almost 13 miles in one hour

How fast can man travel?

On October 28, 1966, Belgium's great Olympic runner, Gaston Roelants, running near Louvain, his home town, covered 12 miles, 1,474 yards in one hour!

Source: Track & Field News; November, 1966; page 1.

1967 Feigner, pitching a softball, strikes out six professional baseball players

By age 21, Eddie Feigner had developed into a pretty good softball pitcher. He had achieved a hefty reputation in the sport; for even against good opposition, he played exhibition ball with only a four-man team: a catcher, a shortstop, and a first baseman, and himself as pitcher. With only four players, *The King and His Court,* as his abbreviated team came to be known, held the field against an opposing full nine. Feigner started on tour in 1946. Since then, Feigner and his three teammates have run up a record of 3,400 victories to 320 defeats.

During this span, Feigner's individual exploits have been notable. *The King* has hurled 530 no-hitters, including 152 perfect games in which nary a single opponent reached first base. His burning fast ball has been clocked at 104 miles per hour. And *the King* has even pitched hitless, scoreless innings while blindfolded!

But his greatest feat was registered on February 18, 1967, while pitching for a group of Hollywood celebrities against a team of major-league baseball all-stars in a softball game sponsored by National Broadcasting Company television. Feigner was a "ringer" on a team that included Steve Allen, James Garner, Bobby Darin, and Don Adams; and the major leaguers in this game did not realize they were facing the finest softball pitcher who ever lived.

Coming in to pitch only when his team was in trouble, Feigner struck out the following players in order: Willie Mays and Willie McCovey of the San Francisco Giants; Brooks Robinson of the Baltimore Orioles; Roberto Clemente and Maury Wills of the Pittsburgh Pirates; and Harmon Killebrew of the Minnesota Twins. Pitching the big ball underhand, and

drawing on his wide repertoire of trick deliveries, Feigner
utterly baffled this galaxy of big-league sluggers. He had the
big boys "eating out of his hand."

Source: *Sport Magazine; November, 1967; pages 46-49.*

1967 Bachler jumps 505 feet on skis

In recent years, ski jumpers have been soaring so far through the air that the term *ski-flying* has come into use. And this term can well be applied to a 22-year-old Austrian named Reinhold Bachler.

On March 12, 1967, Bachler shook hands with destiny. Competing against the greatest of Norwegian flyers who had gathered together on Vikersund-Bakken Hill outside Oslo, Bachler sped down the ramp at about 60 miles an hour. Then, at the bottom of the platform, Reinhold broke out of his crouch and soared into the sky for a world's record leap of 505 feet!

The sailing maneuver necessitates the utmost confidence. The competitor must lay his body over his skis, arms at his sides, and must remain motionless. Should he turn up one of the ends of his skis, it would be just like putting the brakes on a speeding car. He must be aloof to the watching crowd, impervious to the weather, and unaware of all of his surroundings—until his skis hit the ground.

Bachler coordinated all the elements of his jump into one smooth swirl. He landed gently, held himself from falling, and skied to a halt, after sailing more than 168 yards in mid-air—much farther than the length of a football field plus its two end-zones.

(Incidentally, 400 feet is considered a very good ski jump.)

Source: *Ski Magazine; October, 1967; page 40.*

1967 Chichester sails around the world alone on a 53-foot ketch

During the 1920's and 1930's, a spare, simple-looking English real estate magnate turned to flying. Combining skill with daring, Francis Chichester established a number of aerial records in those days. However, one of his attempts led to his being invalided for five years. As soon as he was able to get around again, Chichester attempted a solo flight around the world, crashed into some telegraph poles in Japan, broke 13 bones, and finally looked for his thrills on the ground—or shall we say on the water.

When he was 52, Chichester decided to set forth on the greatest adventure of his life. His boat, the Gipsy Moth IV, a sea-going ketch, 53 feet in length, was normally manned by a crew of six. On August 27, 1966, Francis Chichester sailed off in the Gipsy Moth IV from Plymouth, England, as the lone passenger and the lone crewman. Objective: to sail around the world.

"The only way to live in the full," said the dauntless Englishman, "is doing something which depends on physical action, on the senses, and at the same time on the man-developed parts of the brain." It was to be a harrowing trip, a challenge if he, one man, could manage a vessel that normally required six stalwarts under racing conditions. When he reached the treacherous waters of Cape Horn, squalls as strong as 100 knots an hour rocked his ketch and frigid waves spilled over his deck. Five times his cockpit was flooded, and Chichester was in mortal peril.

Yet against all odds, the man succeeded and Britain paid him homage. Queen Elizabeth was so impressed with the exploit that she knighted him while he was still at sea. In all, Sir Francis covered 28,500 miles in a voyage that took him 226 days. Safely ashore, Sir Francis once again reiterated his philosophy: "It's the effort that counts, not the success." And the trip must certainly stand as one of the greatest physical efforts ever made by a man past fifty.

Source: *Current Biography; December, 1967; pages 5-8.*
"Gipsy Moth Sails The World"; Francis Chichester; Coward-McCann; 1968.

1967 McManus waterskis barefoot for an hour and a half

On May 29, 1967, Paul McManus and his friend scanned
their eyes over the waters of the Hawkesbury River
near Sydney, Australia, and found the calmness to their liking.

The man in the boat began to pull McManus on skis, and hauled him along until Paul got up a proper speed. Then McManus kicked off his skis and skiied along the water barefoot. He maintained this stance for better than one hour and a half—one hour, 30 minutes and 19 seconds, to be exact. A record, of course!

Source: Letter from *The Water Skier* magazine, official publication of the American Water Ski Association; July 17, 1968.

1967 Strawson treads water for 17½ hours

Under the supervision of his trainer, Peter Garner, Peter Strawson, a resident of Lawford in Essexshire, England, set a world's record on July 25–26, 1967, for treading water in a vertical posture. The performance took place in a pool at Warner's Holiday Village in Essexshire. Strawson adhered to the strictest possible rules: no rest periods were allowed; touching the bottom or sides of the pool area was absolutely forbidden. Peter succeeded in treading water for an exhausting 17-1/2 hours.

Source: Manningree & Mistley Standard; December 8, 1972.

1967 Arntz plays a piano almost nonstop for 44 days

No one had ever considered piano-playing a test of endurance—at least, not until Heinz Arntz began playing away in a Dusseldorf cafe on August 18, 1967. Except for two hours' rest each day, Arntz played continuously from mid-August until the first of October. To stay awake for 44 days, with only two hours of sleep each day, is a feat beyond the powers of most humans, no matter of what age or physical condition. But Heinz Arntz—sixty-seven years old—kept awake and plunked away with hardly any surcease for a stretch of 1.056 hours.

He mixed his favorite waltzes and marches into a meaningful and continuous show that began in a German cafe and ended—of all places—in a local fair on New York's Long Island.

In Germany, Arntz's stunt hit the news columns and Arntz himself was badly bitten by the publicity bug. So he had himself and his piano loaded into a truck bound for Bremerhaven, and the old boy kept playing all the way to the pier. There, both he and his piano were put on the steamship *United States,* and Arntz continued to play on as before, entertaining the passengers and the over-night clean-up crew. When the ocean liner docked at New York another truck lugged him and his piano to the Long Island Industrial Fair at Roosevelt, New York.

On October 1st, shortly after noon, Arntz selected his favorite march, "Alte Kameraden," for a finale; and then as he quit, he blandly announced: "From now on, I think I'll play concerts.''

To bask in Arntz's publicity, the F. & M. Schaefer Brewing Co. of New York gave him $1,000.

Source: New York Times; October 2, 1967; page 15, column 7.

1968 Laver wins all four major tennis titles in one year — for the second time

Rodney George Laver of Australia, known to his fans as the Rocket, was generally regarded as the world's best tennis player. Red-haired, left-handed, and wiry, Laver stood only 5 feet 8 inches tall and weighed a mere 150 pounds. Yet he had one of the most powerful serves in the game, and a smashing forehand.

In 1962, when he was 24, the Rocket won the Australian, French, British, and U.S. men's singles championships—the Amateur Grand Slam. The four titles had been held simultaneously only once before in tennis history, by Don Budge of the United States in the 1937–38 season.

The following year Laver turned pro. At first, it appeared as if his great days as a tennis player were over, for in 1963 he lost 21 of his 23 matches. Within a few years, though, Laver regained all his old form; and by 1967, he was the top pro tennis player. The following year, Laver won the four men's singles championships once again, to become the only tennis player in history to achieve the Grand Slam twice.

Source: New York Times Magazine; November 30, 1969; pages 58 ff.

1967 McPeak rides a 32-foot-high unicycle

In 1967, Steve McPeak of Tacoma, Washington, built himself a 32-foot high unicycle that had an intricate gear and pedaling system. This contraption, almost four stories high, had only one drawback. It was so very tall that McPeak had difficulty getting astride it. He solved this problem by building a 35-foot wooden tower from which he could mount the vehicle.

Steve would perch himself atop the unicycle at one tower. Then balancing himself only with his hands, he set out for the opposite tower which was as much as 100 feet away.

Source: *Letter from Dr. and Mrs. Miles S. Rogers, unicycle historians; July 26, 1968.*
Senior Weekly Reader; summer edition, 1967; page 3, column 1.

1968 Knievel, on a motorcycle, jumps over 16 automobiles

From the mountains of Butte, Montana, came Robert Craig Knievel, daredevil stunt rider, who, to dramatize his billing, chose the nickname of "Evel." And Knievel certainly had an eye for the dramatic.

On May 30, 1967, at the Ascot Speedway in Gardena, California, Evel Knievel gunned his Triumph motorcycle and jumped off a ramp at a speed of 80 miles an hour. That allowed him to clear 16 automobiles standing in a row.

To prove the stunt was no fluke, Knievel attempted 16 cars again—four more times, to be exact. Twice he made it.

The other two times proved how dangerous the feat is: once he broke his lower spine, the other time he suffered a brain concussion.

This type of daredeviltry earned the 29-year-old Montanan about $100,000 in 1967. Now Knievel planned a bigger spectacular. The ornamental fountains at *Caesar's Palace,* one of the large hostelries and casinos of Las Vegas, had been advertised as the largest privately owned fountains in the world. On New Year's Day, 1968, Knievel set forth to scale these waterspouts.

A ramp was especially built for him. He took off at 100 miles an hour and catapulted his 198-pound body to a height of 30 feet. He was definitely over the fountains with a leap of 150 feet. But evil pursued Knievel, and as his Triumph motorcycle hit the descending ramp at a speed of 70 miles an hour, the front wheel went askew, and Knievel lost control. He sped along over the neighboring asphalt parking lot for 165 feet, and then wound up in the hospital.

Was Evel daunted? Not so that anybody could make out. Four years later, he cleared 20 cars!

Sources: *Sports Illustrated;* February 5, 1968; pages 60-70.
Current Biography; February 1972; pages 24–26.

1968 Robbins scales a 3,000-foot vertical wall

Royal Robbins operated a paint store in Modesto, California. For kicks, he did mountain climbing. He had negotiated a number of the awesome monoliths of Yosemite Valley; and now, at 32, he was ripe and ready to conquer El Capitan, or specifically the Muir wall of El Capitan, a sheer, vertical facade of 3,000 feet of granite.

On April 21, 1968, Royal Robbins, with a 40-pound duffle bag slung over his shoulder, hammered his first piton into the wall and began his ascent. As the first evening darkened around him, he had reached only 300 feet above the ground. Finding a small ledge, he pounded hooks into the stone and hung a hammock on the wall. At that rate, it was going to take him 10 days to reach the top of the mountain.

It was hard work; it was tedious work. And there were hazards, too; some of the rock wouldn't hold. On one day, Robbins fell and just miraculously saved himself.

For 10 days, Robbins hammered his hooks into that wall of stone and kept climbing, climbing, climbing. Finally, he reached the summit.

Why did he do it? "It's because it's a personal thing with me," answered Robbins.

Source: Letter from Margo McKee, American Alpine Society; August 18, 1968; pages 242-43.

1968 Emma Smith is buried alive for 101 days

For most people, burial in a coffin is the end. For Mrs. Emma Smith, however, it was the beginning of a test of endurance and self-reliance in which she proved that men have no monopoly on courage.

A 38-year-old mother of three from Nottinghamshire, England, Mrs. Smith decided to go underground in June 1968 to bring the duration record back to England (at that time it was held by an Irishman who had stayed underground a mere 61 days).

Mrs. Smith's subterranean venture was sponsored by the Nottingham Instant Help Club, whose members remained on

the scene day and night in case of an emergency. She was buried in an 8-foot coffin, under about 10 tons of earth, at the Skegness Amusement Park in Nottinghamshire.

The coffin was provided with electric lighting and heating. There was a pipe to the surface for food and drink, and a closed-circuit TV hookup so that nurses on the surface could keep in constant touch—also, so that some 50,000 visitors to the Skegness funfair could look at her after paying 1 shilling each for the privilege. Mrs. Smith was able to chat with her husband and her children from time to time by a radio-telephone hookup.

Deep in the earth, Mrs. Smith passed the time knitting, writing long overdue letters to friends and relatives, and working on her life story for a local newspaper. On one occasion, she played bingo with vacationers on the surface. She remained in good spirits most of the time, and only once, in a brief moment of depression that soon passed, was she tempted to ring the alarm bell and come to the surface.

Mrs. Smith emerged from underground on September 17, 1968, after 101 days in her coffin.

Source: Chronicle Advertiser (Mansfield, Nottinghamshire); May 30, 1968;

1968 Beamon broad jumps more than 29 feet

For many years, the long-jump record hovered in the area of 27 feet, with each new mark besting the previous one by only an inch or two. Just as many sports observers had once held

that running the mile in less than four minutes was a physical impossibility, many claimed that 27 to 28 feet was the human limit for long jumping.

Then came the 1968 Olympic Games in Mexico City, where Bob Beamon did to the long-jump pundits what Roger Bannister had done to the brahmins of the mile run.

As a member of the United States Olympic team, Beamon was, of course, an outstanding jumper. In fact, he had set an indoor record of 27 feet, 1 inch, and had made an outdoor jump of 27 feet, 2-3/4 inches.

Despite this, none of the 45,000 spectators at Olympic Stadium were prepared for what they were about to witness on October 18, 1968. Beamon began his running start to the take-off board, and flew off like a shot. Apparently, aided by the thin air of Mexico City, which is situated at an altitude of 7,350 feet above sea level, Beamon soared across the long-jump area with his knees pulled up to his chest and his arms extended sideways.

The onlookers watched in amazement, then broke into wild applause as the stadium's scoreboard flashed confirmation of what they had seen—a jump of 6.90 meters, or 29 feet, 2-1/2 inches. Beamon had surpassed the previous record by nearly two feet!

Source: *New York Times; January 21, 1968;* section V; page 10, column 6; *March 16, 1968;* page 23, column 1; *October 19, 1968;* page 44, column 1

1968 Miller completes a triple-twisting double back somersault on a trampoline

Of all the fancy names used in sport, probably the most odd and esoteric is the term *tri fliffis*, which in trampoline language means a double-back somersault complicated

by three lateral twists, or pirouettes of the body.

Only one athlete in the world is credited with having performed a tri fliffis. He is Wayne Miller of Lafayette, Louisiana, a student at the University of Michigan, and a member of its gymnastic team from 1965 through 1968. Miller, who happens to be a fine diver, became an expert trampolinist, too, bouncing up and down on the nylon web bed. When he performed this rare stunt, Miller catapulted himself about 15 feet high in the air. Then he began his first somersault. During that spin, he began to execute 2⅞ body twists, leaving the remaining half twist for the final somersault of his descent. Midway through the stunt, Miller would draw his knees in toward his chest to accelerate the action for the second somersault without stopping. The whole procedure—which took him hardly more than a second in time—has to be executed with lightning-like rapidity.

The tri fliffis is actually so difficult that no other gymnast in the world has ever succeeded in duplicating Miller's feat.

Source: Letter from Newt Loken, gymnastics coach, University of Michigan; November 28, 1968.

1968 Sheppard rides his motorcycle through a 35-foot tunnel of fire

The "tunnel of fire" is one of the most thrilling of motorcycle stunts. The cyclist must race his machine at full speed through a long series of straw hoops that have been set ablaze.

On September 21, 1968, at the Eurofreeze Trophy stock car meeting at the Rayleigh Stadium in Rayleigh, Essex, England, the Motor Cyclons stunt team put on a fascinating display of expertise and derring-do. Then came the culminating event. While hundreds of spectators screamed in terror and cheered in admiration, the leader of the Motor Cyclons, Dick Sheppard of Gloucester, made the longest fire ride ever recorded—through a burning tunnel 35 feet long.

Source. News Review (Rayleigh, England); September 25, 1968; page 15.

1968 Clara Wise, at age 80, bowls a 209 game

Clara Wise, a vivacious and energetic octogenarian, began bowling in 1941 when she was 53 years old. In 1962, she left her native Kansas and settled in Las Vegas, where she became a member of six different bowling leagues.

In September, 1968, Clara Wise celebrated her 80th birthday with a party at Showboat Lanes. The very next day, at her regular session with the Hair Raisers League at the Charleston Heights Bowl, Clara Wise rolled a 206 game, followed by a 209 game!

Source: Official publication of the Women's International Bowling Congress; September 1968. Sports Illustrated; March 2, 1970.

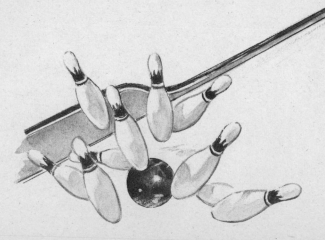

1969 Coghlan sets shoveling record

New Zealand is a big coal-producer. Not surprisingly, the tough, sturdy, competitive New Zealanders who work in the mines take pride in their ability.

In the main coal districts of the Waikato, the Westland, and the Southland, the miners make their work more interesting by competing to surpass each other's production. One contest they enjoy is a race to see who can most quickly fill a half-ton hopper with coal. The more coal a miner heaves in, the harder the task gets, for as it is loaded, the angle of the hopper changes, and each succeeding shovelful must be lifted somewhat higher.

On January 3, 1969, a miner named Don Coghlan, who lives in the town of Reefton, became the world's fastest coal-shoveler. In competition with several other miners, Coghlan took only 56.6 seconds to shovel 1,220 pounds of coal into a hopper—that's about 21 pounds of coal a second. (Coghlan's nearest rival took 10 seconds longer.)

Source: Christchurch (N.Z.) Press; January 4, 1969.
Christchurch (N.Z.) Star; January 3, 1969.

1969 Sinclair walks nearly 216 miles without stopping

John Sinclair is the marathon-walking champion of the world, and he has racked up an impressive series of walking records. He walked from John O'Groats in Scotland to Land's End in

Cornwall, the length of the island of Britain, about 600 miles, in 19 days and 22 hours. In 1967, he walked from Cape Town to Pretoria, a distance of more than 900 miles, in only 23 days.

But John Sinclair's greatest walking feat was performed between April 21 and 23, 1969. The walk took place at the Wingfield Aerodrome, a facility of the South African Navy just outside Simonstown, and it was conducted under official Navy auspices.

The 50-year-old Sinclair began his record-breaking stroll at 5 p.m. on Tuesday, April 21st. Maintaining a steady pace of four miles an hour, and wearing sturdy leather boots that he had carefully broken in some weeks earlier in preparation for the event, he marched around the field's 5.25-mile perimeter, undaunted by the cold, windy rain that began to fall almost immediately after he started.

The rain continued for the next three days, and so did Sinclair. Officers and enlisted men of the South African Navy provided him with food and drink when needed, and served as official observers to ensure that he kept moving at all times and never varied from the measured course around the field.

John Sinclair made his last circuit around Wingfield Aerodrome at 3:42 p.m. on Thursday, April 23. In 47 hours and 42 minutes, he had walked 215 miles 1,670 yards—the greatest feat of marathon walking ever recorded.

Source: Cape Argus (Cape Town, S.A.); April 23, 1969; April 22, 1969; April 16, 1969; December 14, 1968; June 1, 1968; May 18, 1968; March 23, 1968; February 24, 1968.

1969 Sharon Adams sails alone across the Pacific

On July 26, 1969, Sharon Sites Adams, a 39-year-old California housewife, sailed her 31-foot ketch into San Diego harbor.

She was given a warm, emotional welcome by her husband, who is a professional sailing instructor, and by hundreds of enthusiastic friends, relatives, and admirers.

Sharon Adams had just become the first woman ever to sail alone across the Pacific Ocean. She had covered the 5,618-mile distance from her starting point, Yokohama, Japan, to San Diego, in 74 days, 17 hours, 15 minutes.

Source: New York Times; July 26, 1969; page 28 column 7;
Sports Illustrated; August 11, 1969.

1969 Shackelford waterskis more than 818 miles nonstop

Towed in his inboard speedboat *Ye-'Ont II* by relays of friends who kept him supplied during the race with copious quantities of Pepsi-Cola (all told he consumed three cases of the beverage before the end of the marathon), Marvin Shackelford began water-skiing at 10:30 a.m. on Wednesday, August 10, 1969. The race was held around Treasure Island, Kellar Lake, in Tennessee. By midnight, all but five of the 14 starters had dropped out, due to fatigue, cramps, or other mishaps. The remaining competitors—Shackelford among them—circled

Treasure Island all that night. By 7:30 Thursday morning, after completing 79 laps (489.8 miles), Shackelford's last rival had given up.

Shackelford was now the winner, but he still carried on for another 33 laps or 205 miles. By then, he had been on his skis for 31 hours and 20 minutes.

Source: Sports Illustrated; January 12, 1970; pages 67–72. Memphis Appeal; August 12, 1970.

1969 Azzar lies on a bed of nails for 25½ hours

The fakirs of the mysterious East claim to have performed fantastic feats of endurance. But many fakirs are no more than common fakers, and upon investigation it usually

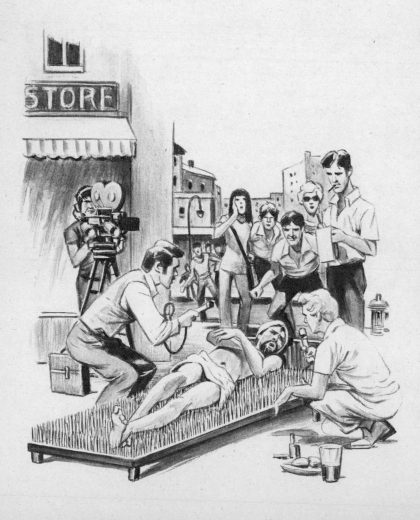

turns out that their purported feats all took place under circumstances that render their claims quite dubious.

In Sydney, Australia, there is a fakir who backed up his amazing claims by performing his feat in the presence of newsmen and numerous other spectators, outside one of Sydney's leading department stores: Walton's, on Park Street.

On the morning of November 20, 1969, bearded Zjane Azzar, clad only in turban and loincloth, gingerly lowered himself into a prone position on a bed of razor-sharp six-inch nails, spaced two inches apart from each other. Throughout that day, the following night, and into the next morning, Azzar remained on his bed of nails, refreshing himself from time to time by smoking a cigarette or by eating a hamburger and some ice cream. During much of this period, he clearly suffered considerable pain. Once his pulse reading was so weak that the attending nurse had to use hot and cold compresses to revive him, and wanted to call the whole thing off.

Azzar refused. He remained stretched out on his bed of nails for a total of 25-1/2 hours, surpassing all previously recorded feats. As Azzar tried to raise himself at the end of his ordeal, he said, "My body has been dead for 14 hours," and then fainted. He was later examined by a doctor who, despite the pattern of deep indentations in Azzar's back, found him weak but physically little damaged.

Source: Sydney Daily Mirror; November 21, 1969.

1970 Teresa Marquis limboes under a six-and-a-half-inch bar

Limbo dancing originated in the West Indies, the home of the Calypso beat. It is most certainly a demanding test of physical coordination.

It was on the West Indian island of St. Lucia, one of the Windward group in the southeastern Carribean, that the world's champion limbo dancer was born in 1946. Her name is Teresa Marquis, and she is a lithe, attractive professional dancer, who with her brother Tunji has played cabarets and nightclubs throughout the British Isles.

In April 1970, Teresa and Tunji were on tour in Northern Ireland. On April 15, while she was visiting a beer distribution plant in Belfast, Teresa was asked if she was good enough to beat the "lowest bar" limbo dancing record, which had been set some years before in New York City when some wraith of a man had limboed under a bar which stood only 6-3/4 inches above the ground.

Never one to turn down a challenge, Teresa responded, knowing that she had often danced under an extremely low bar.

A dance floor was improvised, with a bar fixed atop glasses and beer mats. Someone turned on a phonograph. Two minutes later, Teresa had writhed and wriggled her way under the bar, surpassing the previous record by 1/4 inch.

Source: Daily Express (Irish edition); April 16, 1970.

1970 Dickinson, wearing two artificial legs, bowls a 299 game

No matter how crippling a physical handicap seems to be, there are always people who manage to overcome it. Indeed, some of these courageous, determined individuals succeed in performing feats that would be considered outstanding even if their physical conditions were normal.

Take the inspiring case of Lyman Dickinson, of Watervliet, New York. A few years back, both his legs were amputated, and were replaced with artificial limbs. Dickinson had to learn to walk all over again. Thanks to plenty of guts and hard work, Dickinson trained himself to use his new legs so well that he was once again able to engage actively in fishing, hunting, golf, and bowling.

Though hunting and golf involve a considerable amount of walking, bowling presents an even more difficult obstacle; for to roll a bowling ball properly, one has to start by taking a series of quick steps, and then come to a complete stop just short of the foul line.

On July 2, 1970, at a bowling alley in Albany, New York, Lyman Dickinson rolled a 299 game. As all bowling fans know, this is just one pin short of a perfect score, a feat very, very few bowlers ever attain.

Source: New York Times; December 12, 1972. Letter from Edward L. Marcou, Assistant Public Relations Manager, American Bowling Congress.

1970 Hamilton carries a nine-pound brick 40 miles without dropping it or stopping to rest

Ron D. Hamilton, of Arthur River, Western Australia, is the world's brick-carrying champion. The 6-foot 2-inch farmer tones himself up for this uniquely Australian sport by doing as much as 75 miles of roadwork a week—three to five miles with a brick.

In 1968, Hamilton, then 30 years old, participated in the speed brick-carrying contest in Narrogin, Western Australia. The rules required that contestants cover a course 1 mile 186 yards long with a 9-pound brick in each hand. Hamilton came in first, completing the course in an amazing 6 minutes 27 seconds.

On October 10, 1970, at Wagga Wagga, New South Wales, he went on to win the distance brick-carrying record and a prize of $500. He carried a single brick in his hand—no switching permitted—a distance of 40 miles, surpassing his previous mark of 30 miles, set in 1969.

Source: Robert Hemery and Associates Pty. Ltd.

1970 Rayborn speeds a motorcycle at over 265 miles per hour

On October 16, 1970, Calvin Rayborn of San Diego, California, catapulted his unsupercharged Harley-Davidson Sportster over the Bonneville Salt Flats of Utah. In a little under 10 seconds, he had traversed the one-kilometer course at

266.785 miles per hour. He made the return trip at 264.200 miles per hour, thus averaging 265.492 miles per hour for the two runs.

His 19-foot-long, red, white, and blue machine weighed 500 pounds, was computer-designed, had a streamlined monocoque shell, and had a single twin-cylinder engine powered by stroker fuel.

Source: AMA (American Motorcycle Association) News; December 1970; page 23.

1970 Snyder spits a distance of 25 feet, 10 inches

Every July, the town of Raleigh, Mississippi hosts the national Tobacco Spitting Contest, in which veteran tobacco chewers pit their skills of spitting against one another, both in distance and in accuracy. The achievement of distance, the experts say, depends on the quality of the salivation, the absence of cross-wind, the amount of humidity in the air, and other atmospheric conditions. The coordination of a quick snap of the hip and of the neck is essential.

Don Snyder, a resident of Eupora, won his first prize in 1970 by spitting a distance of 25 feet, 10 inches. In 1971 and 1972, he again won the titles, but he did not surpass his 1970 record.

Source: Smith County (Miss.) Reformer; August 2, 1972; page 1.

1970 Dempsey kicks a record 63-yard field goal

Nothing had been going right for the New Orleans Saints in the 1970 season. The offense was weak, the defense porous, and the kicking off-target.

Oddsmakers gave the Saints little chance of defeating the Detroit Lions on Sunday, November 8. Even the weather had conspired against the young team from the South—it was snowing.

But the Saints played tough defense, and walked off the field at halftime trailing by only 7–6. The New Orleans points had come from the left foot of Tom Dempsey, who had made good on only five of 15 field-goal attempts going into the game.

Actually, it was remarkable that Dempsey could kick at all. The 23-year-old Saint had been born with only half a right foot, and wore a special shoe to give his foot a kicking surface.

In the third quarter, Dempsey kicked another field goal, but Detroit scored a touchdown and stretched its lead to 14–9. The Saints continued to hang in the game, but with only seconds left they were trailing 17–16. They had possession of the ball on their own 44-yard line, and time enough for only one more play.

In desperation, the New Orleans coach sent Dempsey out to attempt a field goal from his own 37-yard line (the ball must be snapped to a point seven yards behind the line of scrimmage to prevent a blocked kick). This was three yards farther from the goal posts than the kickoff point! No one

had ever kicked so long a field goal—the record was 56 yards, set 17 years earlier.

With the snow obscuring the yard markers on the field, Dempsey put all his 264 pounds into the kick, and sent the ball sailing eerily through the snow on a high arc.

Unbelievably, the ball dropped between the uprights 63
yards away. The Saints had upset the Lions 19–17
on the last play of the game!

Source: New York Times; November 9, 1970.

1971 Churchill speeds over the water on a ski at better than 126 miles per hour

On March 28, 1971, 5,000 spectators crowded the Airport Marine Stadium in Oakland, California for a sunny afternoon of inboard dragboat racing. But the highlight of the day proved to be Danny Churchill's courageous—and successful —assault on the world's water-ski speed record. At 3:39 p.m. Churchill set off when the water was choppy and atmospheric conditions were far from ideal.

Towed at the end of a 250-foot line attached to the hydroplane *Crucifier*, Danny bent in a semi-crouch on his single oversized ski, and shot down the quarter-mile course at an almost blinding speed. Undaunted by the merciless shaking his body was put through by the rough water and heavy wind, the daredevil covered the distance in barely seven seconds. He had traveled at an average speed of 126.40 miles per hour—better than two miles per minute, an hour over the previous world's record.

On a backup run made shortly thereafter, as required by the rules, Churchill tracked the same course at 125.69 miles per hour, once again surpassing the previous record.

Source: Bay & Delta Yachtsman; May 1971.

1971 Nicolette Milnes Walker sails alone across the Atlantic

The North Atlantic can be pretty rough on a man alone in a small seacraft. Imagine a lone woman at the mercy of that fierce wind and water!

When she was 28 years old, Britisher Nicolette Milnes Walker, a psychologist by profession, became the first female ever to cross the Atlantic Ocean entirely on her own.

Her daring solo voyage began on June 12, 1971 when she sailed out of the Welsh harbor of Dale in her 30-foot sloop *Aziz*. Making an average distance of 77 miles a day, she sailed steadily westward, arriving in Newport, Rhode Island, on July 26, 1971. She had completed the 3,500-mile voyage in only 45 days.

Sources: New York Times; July 27, 1971; page 39, column 6.
Sports Illustrated; August 9, 1971.

1971 Throne bowls a perfect game at age 12

The youngest person ever to bowl a perfect game was a boy named Matt Throne from Millbrae, California. Matt rolled his 300 game on August 19, 1971, when he was only 12 years and 7 months old.

Source: Letter from Edward L. Marcou, Assistant Public Relations Manager, American Bowling Congress.

1971 Pat Havener packs 90 cans of sardines in 10 minutes

Among the thousands of contests that take place each year, one of the most curious is the World Championship Sardine Packing Contest, which is held every August at Fishermen's Memorial Pier in Rockland, Maine. A regular part of the annual Maine Seafoods Festival, this contest, which reflects the importance of the sardine industry to Maine's economy, attracts numerous entrants from canneries throughout the state.

To pack a sardine, one must pick it up, deftly snip off its head and tail with razor-sharp scissors, and place it neatly in an open sardine can. Whoever packs the most sardines in a 10-minute period receives a cash prize and an engraved trophy from the governor of Maine.

The all-time champion sardine-packer is Mrs. Patricia Havener of Waldoboro, Maine, who, with her mother and sisters, works for the Port Clyde Packing Company in Rockland. In August 1971, when she was 24 years old, Pat Havener packed 90 cans of "number fives" (five sardines to the can) in 10 minutes.

With an overall total of 450 sardines, Pat processed an average of 45 of the shiny little fish each and every minute.

Source: Press Herald (Augusta); August 9, 1971.

1971 Rollings does 17,000 consecutive sit-ups

Sit-ups are a standard form of exercise used in many calisthenics classes. To do a sit-up, one lies on one's back with hands folded behind the head. The idea is to keep the legs stretched flat on the floor and then to raise the rest of the body up, bending the trunk at the waist until the elbows touch

the knees. Generally speaking, 20 or at the most 30 of such sit-ups are all the average man or woman can perform. An individual who has been honed to especially good condition may do 100 sit-ups.

On September 13, 1971, Wayne E. Rollings, a 30-year-old Marine captain stationed at Kaneohe, Hawaii, summoned official witnesses and medical aides to the gymnasium of his military post to authenticate his feat.

Wayne began doing sit-ups, and didn't stop until he had done a total of 17,000, achieving this number in 7 hours 27 minutes.

Source: Sports Illustrated; September 13, 1971.

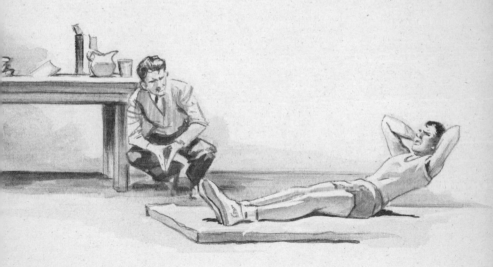

1971 Barnes skates 100 miles in less than five hours and 35 minutes

At the age of 18, Kirt Barnes was hired by the Parks Department of Ann Arbor, Michigan, and was assigned to the Fuller ice-skating rink. If he wanted to hold his job, he was told, he would have to learn to skate.

Barnes learned so well that four years later, at that same Fuller rink, he broke a world's record that had been on the books since 1893! On February 26, 1971, Barnes skated 100 miles without pause in five hours, 34 minutes, and 1.45 seconds. He shattered the previous record by better than one and a half hours.

Source: Ann Arbor News, February 27, 1971.

1972 Woods disc-jockeys for more than 11 days nonstop

Tommy Woods was an undergraduate at William Paterson College in Wayne, New Jersey, and also was active as a disc jockey on WPSC, his college's AM station. In December 1972, he came up with a wild idea: to go on the air and stay on longer than anyone ever had.

Woods began his broadcasting marathon at 8 a.m. on Monday, December 11, 1972, alternating hard-rock music with a steady flow of mellifluous DJ patter. Periodically, a registered nurse stopped in at the studio to check out Woods' physical condition. However, despite fatigue, eyestrain, and increasing hoarseness, Woods remained awake and on the job for more than 11 consecutive days.

Before very long, Tommy became a hero on campus and in the surrounding community. An audience of millions who lived outside WPSC's small listening area vividly followed his progress as reported by TV newsmen in nearby New York City.

Finally, at 4 p.m. on December 22, 1972, Tommy Woods played his last record, said a few final, elated words, and signed off. He had been on the air continuously for a total of 272 hours—a world's record.

Source: Wayne Today; December 17, 1972; page 2.

1972 Yolen flies 50 kites on a single line

Unquestionably, the world's foremost exponent of kite flying is Will Hyatt Yolen of Waterbury, Connecticut.

This was demonstrated at the Fourth Annual International Kitefliers Association Flyoff, which took place at Sandcastle Beach in Sarasota, Florida, on January 15, 1972. Using a 10.0 tuna rig reel, a 120-pound test line, Yolen flew, *at one time*, a wide range of kite types—including a French military model based on those used for communication in the

Franco-Prussian War; numerous Hi-Fliers; a few Korean Beehos; and some varicolored Gayla models. The champ ran up a train of 50 kites on a single line which was 6,400 feet long. The French kite, anchored as a kind of "skyhook," was the first one up—the 49 others followed at 100-foot intervals.

When the 31st kite went up, marking the new record, one of the spectators presented Yolen with a bottle of champagne. He downed some of it, and then, determined to set a mark no one could soon duplicate, he continued to send his kites skyward. He tied the champagne cork to the line between kites numbers 38 and 39, and between the 39th and the 40th he attached the empty champagne bottle.

Source: St. Petersburg (Fla.) Times; January 16, 1972; section 5, page 6, column 8. New York Times; January 15, 1972.

1972 Duhamel speeds at over 127 miles per hour in a snowmobile

The United States Snowmobile Association's 1972 speed trials were held on February 11 at Boonville Airpark in Boonville, N.Y. More than 10,000 spectators turned out for the competition.

Yvon Duhamel of Lasalle, Quebec, entered the open sprint competition with his Ski-Doo X2R, a standard Blizzard sled powered by two 800-cc engines. He shot his snowmobile to the end of the course and returned to the starting point at the fastest speed ever recorded in a sanctioned competition: 127.3 miles per hour.

Source: USSA Sno Track Magazine; March, 1972.

1972 Shoemaker wins 555th stake race

Jockey Willie Shoemaker weighs in at 116 pounds and stands five feet tall. On September 7, 1970, when he was 39 years old, he became the all-time riding champion, breaking the

career mark of 6,032 victories set by Johnny Longden, now retired.

But Shoemaker continued to ride, for there was still another major record to surpass: Eddie Arcaro's mark of 554 stake victories. It took Eddie Arcaro 28 years of hard riding to establish this record, and Willie Shoemaker had been working a long time to beat it. Shoemaker won his first stakes victory on October 26, 1949, riding the horse *A1* in the George Marshall Claiming Handicap.

On March 2, 1972, the big moment came. With 6,296 career victories to his credit, 554 of them stake victories, the 41-year-old jockey was riding *Royal Oak* in the $54,850 San Jacinto Stakes at California's Santa Anita Race Track.

The San Jacinto is a mile event, and there were four other three-year-olds in the race: *Indian, Knightlander, Volume,* and *Right On. Royal Oak* was the odds-on favorite, but he got off to a slow start.

Indian took the lead. At the quarter pole, *Royal Oak* was still behind, and *Indian* was moving ahead at a pretty fast clip. "When I got into my horse," Willie later said, "he responded." In the final stages of the race, *Royal Oak* came up fast to win. He completed the distance in the excellent time of 1:35 1/5.

As a result of this triumph, Willie Shoemaker established a new career stakes mark—555 victories.

Source: New York Times; March 3, 1972; page 45, column 1.

1972 Spitz wins seven Olympic gold medals in swimming

When Mark Spitz arrived in Munich, West Germany for the 1972 Olympic Games, the whole world was watching him. The dark, handsome, powerfully built Spitz had already established himself as the most outstanding swimmer of modern times. He had been swimming since early childhood, and set his first U.S. record in 1960—which still stands—in a 50-yard butterfly competition for nine- and ten-year olds.

Spitz, who lives in Carmichael, California, had won two gold medals at the 1968 Olympic Games in Mexico City, and at various times had broken 28 world freestyle and butterfly records. In 1971 alone, he had won four national and two collegiate championships in the United States, and had set seven world and two U.S. records.

For the 1972 Olympics, Spitz was entered in four individual competitions and three relay events. He had a chance to win seven gold medals, two more than anyone had ever won at a single session of the Olympic Games.

All the spectators at Munich's 9,000-seat Schwimhalle were aware of this record-shattering possibility as Spitz leapt into the pool for his first test, the 200-meter butterfly, on the afternoon of August 28, 1972. Spitz reached the finish line first, beating the world record which he himself had set several weeks before at the U.S. Olympic Trials in Chicago.

A few hours later, as a member of the winning U.S. team in the 400-meter freestyle relay, Spitz won his second gold medal. The next evening, finishing first in the 200-meter freestyle, he won his third.

Spitz won two more medals on September 1: the 100-meter butterfly, in which he set a new world record, and the 800-meter freestyle relay, in which he anchored the winning U.S. team. On September 3, by winning the 100-meter freestyle, Spitz became the first Olympic athlete ever to garner so many gold medals at one Olympiad.

Finally, on September 4, swimming the butterfly leg for the U.S. team in the 400-meter medley relay, the 22-year-old Spitz won his seventh medal.

Source: Time; September 11, 1972; pages 58–67. Newsweek; September 1972; pages 67–68. Current Biography; October; 1972; pages 37–39.

1972 Roberts spits a watermelon seed 38 feet, 8-3/4 inches

Among the many weird championships held throughout the world which are on the fringe of athletic performance, few are quite as nutty as the world championship watermelon-seed spitting contest held at Pardeeville, Wisconsin, on September 12, 1972. The contest is open to competitors of both sexes and all ages. Only tobacco chewers are disqualified.

At this to-do, one Lee Roberts of Rio, Wisconsin, projected a melon seed from his lips the incredible distance of 38 feet, 8-3/4 inches.

Source: Letter from R. H. Thompson, Editor, Pardeeville Times.

1972 Berger shoots two perfect scores in archery — back to back

The point score in U.S. archery is, naturally, highest for a hit on the 9.6-inch-diameter bull's eye, and lowest for one on the outermost of the concentric rings. In a standard archery tournament, which consists of a series of rounds at different distances from the target, a perfect score is 300.

Only one man in the history of modern archery has ever shot two perfect 300 scores back-to-back. Competing in a major sanctioned tournament in Las Vegas, Nevada, in January 1972, Vic Berger turned the trick. Moreover, at that same meet, Berger shot a record score of 899 out of a possible 900, a feat he had performed two years earlier in Las Vegas.

Source: Letter from Fred Schuette, Executive Secretary, American Archery Council; January 25, 1973.

1973 Miller shoots a 63 in final round of U.S. Golf Open

When in June of 1973, the pros gathered in Oakmont, Pennsylvania, for the U.S. Open, the name of Johnny Miller was familiar to none but the most dedicated of golf fans. The 26-year-old linksman had never before won a major tourney, and was accorded little chance of winning this most prestigious classic.

Yet on the first day, Miller came back to the clubhouse with a 69, two strokes under par, and only two strokes off the lead. The next day, Johnny came through with a par 71, but this performance only succeeded in setting him back another stroke behind the leader. When he skyrocketed to a 76 on the third round, what slim chance he had of winning now seemed to have completely vanished.

So when Miller began his final leg on Sunday the 17th, six strokes and 35 players separated him from the lead. As the crowds swarmed around such golf immortals as Gary Player, Arnold Palmer, and Jack Nicklaus, the unknown Miller quietly set out on the most incredible round in history.

Coming in *four under par!* on the first nine holes, Miller was now one-under par for the tourney. A dazzling 19-foot putt gave him a birdie on the 11th hole and edged him still closer to the top, as the leaders, unnerved by Miller's charge, started to falter. When Miller dropped in a 15-footer on the next hole, he put himself in the lead. When he parred the 18th, the stunned crowd had found a new hero, and the Open had a new champion.

Miller's five-under-par 279 for the difficult 72 holes was a

new course record. His final 63—an unbelievable 8 under par—was a new course record, a new tournament record, and was likely the finest round of pressure golf ever played.

Source: Sports Illustrated; June 25, 1973; pages 16–21.

INDEX

INDEX